AIRLINE TRAVEL MADE EASY

AIRLINE TRAVEL MADE EASY

SUZANNE J. MORIN

At-home Publications

Rockwood, Ontario

COPYRIGHT © 1998 Suzanne J. Morin

Published By   AT-HOME Publications, R.R #1, Rockwood, Ontario N0B 2K0

For a completed list of titles in print visit our website at: www.at-homepublications.com

Canadian Cataloguing in Publication Data

Morin, Suzanne J., 1959-
    Airline Travel Made Easy

ISBN 1-894125-08-8

    1. Air travel--Handbooks, manuals, etc. I. Title.

HE9768.M67 1998   **910' .2'02**   **C98-900791-X**

Design Layout and Editor: Pamela Lucier
Contributing Editor: C. Stuart Hunter
Cover Design and Graphics: Catherine Bould
Final Proof and Editing: Matthew Bunch

Printed in Canada

Dedication

To my loving husband, Danny, who never stopped believing in me.

Table of Contents

Acknowledgements

My thanks to all the travellers I encountered over the years while I was working with the airlines. Without their concerns, questions, and comments this book would never have been written. In addition, I would like to thank all the people I worked with for their help, encouragement, stories, and friendship that made working with the airline such a joy. I would also like to thank Aranka K. Torok, Emese Torok, Katalin Monson, Brigitte Garito, for their advice and inspiration; Susan Smyth, Pam Lucier, Catherine Bould, C. Stuart Hunter, Matthew Bunch for all their hard work; and Daiva L. Blynas. Last but not least, special thanks to Arleen Rogers for her technical help with the inflight training part of this book.

INTRODUCTION

Airline travel can be confusing and frustrating. However, I can help make your journey easy and enjoyable. When planning a trip, whether from your home or office, you will be subject to many rules and regulations such as fares, baggage, schedules, customs, documents, health insurance, meals, and special services, to name a few. This may seem confusing, but relax, help is on the way.

I have worked for a major Canadian airline for sixteen years and having worked in all sales capacities of the airline industry. I know what can go wrong and what **should** go right. That is why I have put this book together. I will try and give you, the traveller, an insight into what you should be aware of. In this way, I hope to make travelling easier for you.

Most airlines have the same basic rules and policies, but there are differences. It is your responsibility to ask and understand the rules for the carrier that you are using. This can be done when you make a reservation, either with the airline or with a travel agent; it is your responsibility to ask the necessary questions pertaining to your travel needs and concerns. A reservation agent with a specific airline can only advise you on their policies. A travel agent can not possibly be expected to know or anticipate all of the customers' questions and concerns.

When you understand what to expect and what you as a traveller are entitled to, when you realize the complexities involved, when you see how much common sense prevails, much of the stress will be removed and flying will be easier.

I have tried to address the major concerns and questions I encountered while working at the airport, specifically in the reservations office, in the hopes that you will have the majority of your questions answered. So settle in your favorite chair and read on.

Suzanne J. Morin

MAKING TRAVEL PLANS
Chapter 1: Fares

Perhaps you have a destination in mind or maybe you haven't settled on one yet. Either way, understanding fares will allow you to get the best price and may even be a determining factor on when and where you travel. Fares can be frustrating for the customer. To the customer, "How much will it cost to fly to Miami?" may seem like a fairly simple question, but it's not as straightforward a question as it sounds. With the increasing need for airlines to be competitive and grab your business from another carrier, airlines have come up with all kinds of different rules, restrictions, and seasons of travel which govern fares.

Gone are the days when airlines had three simple fares: First class, Business class, and Coach. These classes have been replaced with a myriad of fares that can take up to three pages in a computer system! If you have worked on a computer system before you will realize that three pages is indicative of many fares. When quoting a fare, an agent will need to know answers to questions like, "When are you travelling?" or "How long will you be away?" and "Do you have time to advance book your reservation by fourteen days?" These are not questions aimed at satisfying the agent's curiosity or a way of prying into your personal affairs. Instead, these questions are asked so that the best possible fare can be quoted.

Usually a customer will inquire about the fare first and, consequently, the conversation will frequently go like this:

Customer:	"I would like to know what it will cost to fly to Vancouver."
Agent:	"Can you tell me when you would like to travel?"
Customer:	"When the fare is the cheapest."
Agent:	"Well, there are several fares depending on when you travel. Do you have time to advance book by fourteen days?"
Customer:	"Yes. I won't be travelling until the summer."
Agent:	"Can you be specific as to the month?"

By this time the customer is getting impatient. After all, he/she just wanted the cost of a fare! Why all the questions? Unless you give the agent more information or specific dates you can be quoted the wrong fare. So **please**, when you are inquiring about the cost, try to give the agent at least the month, if not the actual dates, that you want to travel.

The other frustrating thing about fares is availability. Each fare is booked in the reservations system according to **booking class code** and depending on the dollar value of the ticket there will only be a certain number of seats allocated to be sold at that level. The general rule is this: The lower the fare the fewer seats allocated. For example, on an aircraft that holds one hundred and twenty-one seats in Coach there may be fifty seats allocated to be sold at the lowest fare, sixty seats for the next lowest fare, and so on. That is why when you call to book the "$199.00" fare to Los Angeles, you may be told that the fare is sold out, but the "$299.00" fare is still available. All this means is that the fifty seats allotted be to sold at the lower fare level have been booked and, therefore, to travel on the same date and flight you will have to pay the higher fare.

Have you ever been on a plane and wondered why the person sitting next to you paid less for their ticket than you did for yours? After all, you are on the same airplane, travelling to the same destination, so why the difference? It is not because the agent who made out your ticket was incompetent or that the airline charges whatever to whomever they feel. It is because the person beside you made their reservation at an earlier time than you did and managed to secure one of the "seat sale" fares. If cost is the major factor influencing your choice of vacation site, you should note that off-season (i.e. Miami in July, Paris in February, Barbados in August, etc.) trips offer the lowest fares. In addition, if your dates are approximate, the travel agent can check dates before and after your planned trip is supposed to take place to determine when the rates are lower.

Yet another consideration with fares is restrictions. Restrictions include minimum booking dates, cancellation penalties, and the minimum and maximum stay.

Lower priced fares will usually require booking in advance by a certain number of days - with the exception of special promotional fare, and they will vary according to the airline and the fare. Usually this will entail advance booking your reservation by seven to twenty-one days. For example, a fare that has a seven day advance booking means that between the time you make your reservation and the date you travel, you must have at least seven days in between. Otherwise, you pay a higher fare. Payment will also be required at least seven days in advance of the travel date, or within twenty-four hours of making your reservation. It is important that you understand these two elements of your booking in order to avoid your file being cancelled by the airline. Also, with a reduced fare there is almost always a cancellation fee. This means that once you have paid for your ticket, you will be charged a specific fee if you cancel your reservation.

Cancellation penalties can range from fifty dollars to the entire value of the ticket. If you want to change your reservation for any reason the same cancellation fee will usually apply. Since these fees differ considerably between airlines, make sure you know what the penalties are before you pay for your ticket. While I was working at the airport ticket counter, I frequently encountered passengers wanting to change their reservations on one of these special fares, only to be told it would cost them additional funds. The response was usually one of surprise. It could be that the agent who booked their reservation never advised them of the penalties, or the passengers didn't understand the rules, but regardless, it caused the passenger and the airline a fair amount of difficulty. I should mention here that most airlines and travel agencies are required to put a notation in the passenger file stating which rules were mentioned along with the date and agent's name. So if you are ever in doubt, have the airline pull up your file and see what notations are included.

The last restriction to be considered regarding the price of your trip is the minimum/maximum stay requirements, which are self-explanatory. You will have to stay an agreed minimum stay (such as three days) and will have to return by a certain date meeting the maximum allowed days. Therefore, a fare having a seven-to-sixty day rule simply means you will have to be away at least seven days (not including departure date) and will have to return no later than sixty days after departure.

Having to be away a minimum of one Friday or Saturday night is a very common minimum stay requirement. Most travellers are away for only a few days and this rule will allow them to take advantage of a reduced air fare. However, I can not stress enough how important it is to know and understand the rules pertaining to your fare. For example, you give your travel agent a set of travel dates (leaving on a Friday and returning four days later); you are quoted a reduced rate and are quite happy. You are told you can change your reservation but it must be paid for within twenty-four hours. No problem. You pay for it right away. The next day (knowing you can change the ticket without penalty) you come back and tell the agent you still want to travel for the same amount of days, but you would like to leave on the Saturday instead. The agent checks your reservation and tells you that to travel at that same fare level you have to be away a minimum of one Friday night, which you no longer have. So you end up paying a higher fare.

I agree that you, the traveller, should be advised about the basic rules such as the minimum/maximum stay, the ticket deadline, and the change/ cancellation fees by the booking agent, but you should also not take anything for granted. Any reduced fare is such because there are certain restrictions that make the customer "work," so to speak, to qualify for that fare.

TRAVEL CHECK

Its all fare game so remember to:

√   reserve your seat 7 to 21 days in advance for lower fare

√   there is a penalty for cancellation

√   remember minimum/maximum stay rule

Chapter 2: Travel Agencies & Tourism Associations

Now that you understand the intricacies of fares, you will be more able to estimate where and when you will be able to travel based on what you can afford. This chapter will provide you with a list, in alphabetical order by Province and Territory, of Canada-wide travel agencies and associations, along with an alphabetical list of similar agencies in the United States and abroad. I compiled these lists in the hopes that you may find them useful in planning your travel itinerary. Airline companies and a list of toll-free numbers for hotels and car rental agencies are also listed for your convenience. For further assistance in planning your trip refer to Appendix C for websites concerning all your travel needs.

Canadian Tourism Associations and Travel Agencies

Alberta Economic Development & Tourism
Tourism, Trade & Investment
Commerce Place, 10155-102 St., **Edmonton**, AB T5J 4L6
403/427-2280; Fax: (403) 427-1700

Alberta Hotel Association
#401, 5241 Calgary Trail South, **Edmonton**, Alberta T6H 5G8
(403) 436-6112 or fax: (403) 436-5404

Alberta League for Environmentally Responsible Tourism

P.O. Box 1288, **Rocky Mountain House**, Alberta T0M 1T0

(403) 845-4667 or fax: (403) 845-5377

Alberta Tourism Partnership Corp.

#500, 999 - 8 Street SW, **Calgary**, Alberta T2R 1J5

(403) 297-2957 or fax: (403) 297-5068

URL: http://www.atp.ab.ca/

Calgary Convention & Visitors Bureau

237 - 8 Avenue SE, **Calgary**, Alberta T2G 0K8

(403) 263-8510 or fax: (403) 262-3809

Toll Free: 1-800-661-1678

Motel Association of Alberta

#202, 10335 - 178 Street, **Edmonton,** Alberta T5S 1R5

(403) 944-1199 or fax: (403) 455-6675

Ministry of Small Business, Tourism & Culture

Tourism Division, 1117 Wharf St., **Victoria,** B.C. V8W 2Z2

250/356-6363 (Tourism); Fax: 250/356-8248

British Columbia & Yukon Hotels Association

948 Howe Street, 2nd Floor, **Vancouver**, BC V6Z 1N9

(604) 681-7164 or fax: (604) 681-7649

Toll Free: 1-800-663-3153

URL: http://www.fleethouse.com/fhcanada/bcacco.htm

Cariboo Tourism Association

190 Yorsten St., P.O. Box 4900, **Williams Lake**, BC V2G 2V8

(250) 392-2226 or fax: (250) 392-2838

Toll Free: 1-800-663-5885

Email: cariboo@netshop.ca

Council of Tourism Associations of British Columbia

P.O. Box 28005, RPO Harbour Centre,**Vancouver**, BC V6B 5L8

(604) 685-5956 or fax: (604) 730-4801

Email: jimmann@uniserve.com

URL: http://www.fleethouse.com/fhcanada/bcacco.htm

High Country Tourism Association

#2 , 1490 Pearson Place, **Kamloops**, BC V1S 1J9

(250) 372-7770 or fax: (250) 828-4656

Kootenay Country Tourist Association

610 Railway Street, **Nelson**, BC V1L 1H4

(250) 352-6033 or fax: (250) 352-1656

Toll Free: 1-800-661-6603

Email: kcta@worldtel.com

URL: http://travel.bc.ca.kootenay

North by Northwest Tourism Association

3736 - 16th Ave., P.O. Box 1030, **Smithers**, BC V0J 2N0

(250) 847-5227 or fax: (250) 847-7585

Okanagan Similkameen Tourism

1332 Water Street, **Kelowna**, BC V1Y 9P4

(250) 860-5999 or fax: (250) 861-7493

Email: osta@awinc.com

Peace River Alaska Highway Tourism

10631 - 100th St., P.O. Box 6850, Station Main, **Fort St. John**, BC V1J 4J3

250) 785-2544 or fax: (250) 785-4424

Rocky Mountain Visitor's Association

495 Wallinger Ave., P.O. Box 10, **Kimberley**, BC V1A 2Y5

(250) 427-4838 or fax: (250) 427-3344

Tourism Association of Vancouver Island

#302, 45 Bastion Square, **Victoria** BC V8W 1J1

(202) 382-3551 or fax: (250) 382-3523

Tourism Vancouver/Greater Vancouver Convention & Visitors Bureau

Two Bentall Centre, #210, 200 Burrard St., **Vancouver**, BC V6C 3L6

(604) 682-2222 or fax: (604) 682-1717

Vancouver Coast & Mountains Tourism Region

#204, 1755 Broadway West, **Vancouver**, BC V6J 4S5

(604) 739-9011 or fax: (604) 739-0153

Toll Free: 1-800-667-3306

Email: vcm.tourism@mindlink.bc.ca

URL: http://travel.bc.ca

WorldHomes Holiday Exchange

1707 Platt Crescent, **North Vancouver**, BC V7J 1X9

(604) 987-3262 or fax: (604) 987-3262

Email: jgraber@direct.ca

Manitoba Industry, Trade & Tourism

Tourism Initiative; 155 Carlton St., 6th Fl., **Winnipeg**, Manitoba R3C 3H8;
204/945-3796; Toll Free: 1-800-665-0040, ext. TH6; Fax: 204/945-1354

Manitoba Hotel Association

#1505, 155 Carlton Street, **Winnipeg**, Manitoba R3C 3H8

(204) 942-0671 or fax: (204) 942-6719

Tourism Industry of Manitoba Inc.

#104, 1670 Portage Avenue, **Winnipeg**, Manitoba R3C 0C9

(204) 774-8406 or fax: (204) 774-8420

Email: tourism@solutions.mb.ca

Tourism Winnipeg

#320, 25 Forks Market Road, **Winnipeg**, Manitoba R3C 4S8

(204) 943-1970 or fax: (204) 942-4043

Toll Free: 1-800-665-0204

Email: wpginfo@tourism.winnipeg.mb.ca

URL: www.tourism.winnipeg.mb.ca/

Department of Economic Development & Tourism

Tourism Directorate, Centennial Bldg., 670 King St., 5th Fl.,

P.O. Box 6000, **Fredericton** NB E3B 5H1,

506/453-4283; Fax: 506/453-7127

URL: http://www.gov.nb.ca/tourism/index.htm

Fredericton Visitor & Convention Bureau

P.O. Box 130, **Fredericton**, New Brunswick E3B 4Y7

(506) 452-9508 or fax: (506) 452-9509

Email: tourism@darwin.nbnet.nb.ca

Tourism Industry Association of New Brunswick

Prospect Place, #206, 191 Prospect Street,

Fredericton, New Brunswick E3B 2T7

(506) 458-5646 or fax: (506) 459-3634

Department of Tourism, Culture & Recreation

Confederation Bldg, P.O. Box 8700, **St. John's** NF AIB 4J6; 709/729-0662

Tourism and Craft Development, Confederation Bldg, P.O. Box 8700, St. John's NF A1B 4J6; 709/729-0928; Fax: 709/729-0662

Tourism Industry Association of Newfoundland & Labrador
107 LeMarchant Road, P.O. Box 13516, **St. John's**, Newfoundland A1B 4B8
(709) 722-2000 or fax: (709) 722-8104
Toll Free: 1-800-563-0700
Email: dlough@bridges.entnet.nf.ca

Department of Resources, Wildlife & Economic Development
Parks & Tourism Division
#600, Scotia Center Bldg.; Box 21 5102-50 Ave., **Yellowknife** NT X1A 3S8
403/873-7420, 7134; Fax: 403/873-0114

Arctic Coast Tourism Association
P.O. Box 91, **Cambridge Bay**, NT X0C 0C0
(403) 983-2224 or fax: (403) 983-2302

Baffin Tourism
P.O. Box 1450, **Iqaluit**, NT X0A 0H0
(819) 979-6551 or fax: (819) 979-1261

Big River Tourism Association
P.O. Box 185, **Hay River**, NT X0E 0R0
(403) 874-2422 or fax: (403) 874-2027

Nahanni-Ram Tourism Association

P.O. Box 177, **Fort Simpson**, NT X0E 0N0

(403) 695-3182 or fax: (403) 695-2511

Northern Frontier Visitor Association

#4, 4807-49th Street, **Yellowknife**, NT X1A 3T5

(403) 873-4262 or fax: (403) 873-3654

Email: nfva@netnorth.com

Northwest Territories Hotel's Association

Yellowknife Inn, P.O. Box 490, **Yellowknife**, NT X1A 2N4

(403) 873-2601 or fax: (403) 873-2602

Nunavut Tourism

P.O. Box 1450, **Iqaluit**, NT X0A 0H0

(819) 979-6551 or fax: (819) 979-1261

Toll Free: 1-800-491-7910

Email: nunatour@nunanet.com

URL: http://nunanet.com/~nunanet.com

Sahtu Tourism Association

P.O. Box 115, **Norman Wells**, NT X0E 0V0

(403) 587-2054 or fax: (403) 587-2935

Tourism Industry Association of the Northwest Territories
#2, 4807 - 49th Street, **Yellowknife**, NT X1A 3T5
(403) 873-2122 or fax: (403) 873-3654

Travel Keewatin
P.O. Box 328, **Rankin Inlet**, NT X0C 0G0
(819) 645-2618 or fax: (819) 645-2320

Nova Scotia Economic Renewal Agency, Tourism Nova Scotia
1800 Argyle St., P.O. Box 519, **Halifax**, NS B3J 2R7
902/424-8920; Fax: 902/424-0582

Cape Breton Tourist Association
10 Keltic Drive, **Sydney**, Nova Scotia B1S 1P5
(902) 539-9876 or fax: (902) 539-8430

Evangeline Trail Tourism Association
5518 Prospect Road, **New Minas**, Nova Scotia B4N 3K8
(902) 681-1645 or fax: (902) 681-2747

Hotel Association of Nova Scotia
P.O. Box 473, Stn M, **Halifax**, Nova Scotia B3J 2P8
(902) 443-3635 or fax: (902) 457-3304

Tourism Halifax

P.O. Box 1749, **Halifax**, Nova Scotia B3J 3A5

(902) 421-6448 or fax: (902) 421-2842

Tourism Industry Association of Nova Scotia

#402, 1800 Argyle Street, **Halifax**, Nova Scotia B3J 3N8

(902) 423-4480 or fax: (902) 422-0184

Ontario Tourism Partnership

c/o Alberta Economic Development & Tourism, 10155-102 St., **Edmonton** ON T5J 4L6; 403/531-4671

Ministry of Economic Development, Trade & Tourism
Business Development & Tourism Division

 Hearst Block, 900 Bay St., **Toronto** ON M7A 2E1

416/325-6666; Fax: 416/325-6688

Accommodation Motel Ontario Association

347 Pido Road, RR#6, **Peterborough**, Ontario K9J 6X7

(705) 745-4982 or fax: (705) 745-4983

Toll Free: 1-800-461-1972

Email: motels@oncomdis.on.ca

Algoma Kinniwabi Travel Association

#1, 553 Queen Street East, Sault **Ste Marie**, Ontario P6A 2M3

(705) 254-4293 or fax: (705)254-4892

Toll Free: 1-800-263-2541

Almaguin-Nipissing Travel Association

P.O. Box 351, **North Bay**, Ontario P1B 8H5

(705) 474-6634 or fax: (705) 474-9271

Toll Free: 1-800-387-0516

Burlington Visitor & Convention Bureau

1340 Lakeshore Road, **Burlington**, Ontario L7S 1Y2

(905) 634-5948 or fax: (905) 634-7220

Cambridge Visitor & Convention Bureau

531 King Street East, **Cambridge**, Ontario N3H 3N4

(519) 653-1424 or fax: (519) 653-1734

Toll Free: 1-800-749-7560

Cochrane Timiskaming Travel Association

76 McIntyre Rd., P. O. Box 920, **Schumacher**, Ontario P0N 1G0

(705)360-1989 or fax: (705)268-5526

Toll Free: 1-800-461-3766

Convention & Visitors Bureau of Windsor

#103, 333 Riverside Drive West, **Windsor**, Ontario N9A 5K4

(519) 255-6530 or fax: (519) 255-6192

Cornwall & Seaway Valley Tourism

231 Augustus Street, **Cornwall,** Ontario K6J 3W2

(613) 938-4748 or fax: (613) 938-4751

Toll Free: 1-800-937-4748

Email: dmurray@cnwl.igs.net

URL: http://www.visit.cornwall.on.ca

The Georgian Triangle Tourist Association &Convention Bureau

601 First Street, **Collingwood**, Ontario L9Y 4L2

(705) 445-7722 or fax: (705) 444-6082

Greater Hamilton Tourism & Convention Services

One James Street South, 3rd Floor, **Hamilton**, Ontario L8P 4R5

(905) 546-4222 or fax: (905) 546-4107

Hostelling International - Canada

#400, 205 Catherine Street, **Ottawa**, Ontario K2P 1C3

(613) 237-7884 or fax: (613) 237-7868

Hotel Association of Canada Inc.

#1016, 130 Albert Street, **Ottawa**, Ontario K1P 5G4

(613) 237-7149 or fax: (613) 238-3878

Huronia Tourism Association

Simcoe County Building, **Midhurst**, Ontario L0L 1X0

(705) 726-9300 or fax: (705) 726-3991

Kitchener-Waterloo Area Visitor & Convention Bureau

2848 King Street East, **Kitchener**, Ontario N2A 1A5

(519) 748-0800 or fax: (519) 748-6411

Toll Free: 1-800-265-6959

London Visitors & Convention Bureau

300 Dufferin Avenue, **London**, Ontario N6B 1Z2

(519) 661-5000 or fax: (519) 661-6160

Metropolitan Toronto Convention & Visitors Association

#590, 207 Queen's Quay West, P.O. Box 126, **Toronto**, Ontario M5J 1A7

(416) 203-2600 or fax: (416) 203-6753

Info Line: (416)203-2500

Toll Free 1-800-363-1990

Muskoka Tourism

RR #2, **Kilworthy**, Ontario P0E 1G0

(705) 689-0660 or fax: (705) 689-7118

Toll Free: 1-800-267-9700

Niagara Falls Canada Visitor & Convention Bureau

5433 Victoria Avenue, **Niagara Falls**, Ontario L2G 3L1

(905) 356-6061 or fax: (905) 356-5567

Toll Free: 1-800-563-2557

Email: nfcvcb@niagara.com

North of Superior Tourism Association

1119 East Victoria Avenue, **Thunder Bay**, Ontario P7C 1b7

(807) 626-9420 or fax: (807) 626-9421

Toll Free: 1-800-265-3951

Email: nosta@lakeheadu.ca

Northern Ontario Tourist Outfitters Association

#408, 269 Main Street West, **North Bay**, Ontario P1B 2T8

(705) 472-5552 or fax: (705) 472-0621

Email: noto@onlink.net

URL: http://virtualnorth.com/noto/

Ontario Convention & Visitors Association

#301, 250 Consumers Road, **Toronto**, Ontario M2J 4V6

(416) 494-1440 or fax: (416) 495-8723

Email: base@onramp.ca

(705) 254-4293 or fax: (705) 254-4892

Ontario East Tourism Association
RR#1, **Landsdowne**, Ontario KOE 1L0
(613) 659-4300 or fax: (613) 659-4306
Toll Free: 1-800-567-3278

Ontario Hostelry Institute
#213, 300 Adelaide Street East, **Toronto**, Ontario M5A 1N1
(416) 363-3401 or fax: (416) 363-3403

Ontario Private Campground Association
RR#5, **Owen Sound**, Ontario N4K 5N7
(519) 371-3393 or fax: (519) 371-5315

Ontario Ski Resorts Association
#22, 850 Tapscott Road, **Toronto**, Ontario M1X 1N4
(416) 321-2252 or fax: (416) 321-2336

Ontario Hotel & Motel Association
#8 - 201, 2600 Skymark Avenue, **Mississauga**, Ontario L4W 5B2
(905) 602-9650 or fax: (905) 602-9654
Toll Free: 1-800-387-0010

Ontario's Sunset Country Travel Association
P.O. Box 647, **Kenora**, Ontario P9N 3X6
(807) 468-5853 or fax: (807) 468-5484

Info Line: 1-800-665

Toll Free: 1-800-461-6020

Ottawa Tourism & Convention Association

#1800, 130 Albert Street, **Ottawa**, Ontario K1P 5G4

(613) 237-5150 or fax: (613) 237-7339

Info Line: (613)237-5158

Toll Free: 1-800-363-4465

Peterborough Kawartha Tourism & Convention Bureau

175 George Street North, **Peterborough**, Ontario K9J 3G6

(705) 742-2201 or fax: (705) 742-2494

Toll Free: 1-800-461-6424

Rainbow Country Travel Association

Cedar Point Mall, 1984 Regent St. South, **Sudbury**, Ontario P3E 5S1

(705) 522-0104 or fax: (705) 522-3132

Toll Free: 1-800-465-6655

Resorts Ontario

10 Peter Street North, P.O. Box 214, **Orillia**, Ontario L3V 6S1

(705) 325-9115 or fax: (705) 325-7999

Toll Free: 1-800-363-7227

Sarnia/Lambton Visitor & Convention Bureau
224 North Vidal Street, **Sarnia**, Ontario N7T 5Y3
(519) 336-3278 or fax: (519) 336-3278
Toll Free: 1-800-265-0316

Sault Ste. Marie Hospitality & Travel
99 Foster Drive, 3rd Floor, **Sault Ste. Marie**, Ontario P6A 5X6
(705) 759-5432 or fax: (705) 759-2185

Sudbury Convention & Visitors Service
P.O. Box 5000, Stn. A, **Sudbury**, Ontario P3A 5P3
(705) 674-3141 or fax: (705) 671-8145

Tourism Brantford
3 Sherwood Drive, **Brantford**, Ontario N3T 1N3
(519) 751-9900 or fax: (519) 759-5975
Toll Free: 1-800-265-6299

Tourism Industry Association of Canada
#1016, 130 Albert Street, **Ottawa**, Ontario K1P 5G4
(613) 238-3883 or fax: (613) 238-3878
Email: tiac@achilles.net
URL: http://www.achilles.net/~tiac/homepage.html

Tourism Stratford

88 Wellington Street, P.O. Box 818, **Stratford**, Ontario N5A 6W1

(519) 271-5140 or fax: (519) 273-1818

Toll Free: 1-800-561-7926

Tourism Thunder Bay

500 Donald Street East, **Thunder Bay**, Ontario P7E 5V3

(807) 623-3768 or fax: (807) 623-3768

Info Line: (807)346-4636

Toll Free: 1-800-667-8386

Travellers' Aid Society of Metropolitan Toronto

Room B23, Union Station, **Toronto**, Ontario M5J 1E6

(416) 366-7788 or fax: (416) 366-0829

Department of Economic Development & Tourism, Tourism PEI

Annex 1, West Royalty Industrial Park, 1 First Avenue.

Charlottetown, PEI C1B 1B0

902/368-5540; Fax: 902/368-4438

Hotel/Motel Association of Prince Edward Island

455 University Avenue, **Charlottetown**, PE I C1A 4NA

(902) 566-3137 or fax: (902) 368-3806

Travel Association of Prince Edward Island
64 Great George Street, P.O. Box 2050, **Charlottetown**, PEI C1A 7N7(902)
566-5008 or fax: (902) 368 -3605
URL: http://www.gov.pe.ca/conv/tiapei.html

Tourisme Québec
#329, 2, Place Québec, **Québec**, PQ G1R 2B5
418/643-5959; Toll Free: 1-800-363-7777
Fax: 418/646-8723

Institut de Tourisme et D'Hotellerie du Quebec
401, rue de Rigaud, **Montreal**, Quebec H2L 4P3
(514) 282-5108
Ligne sans frais: 1-800-361-5111

L'Association Des Hoteliers Du Quebec/Quebec Hotel Association
Pavillon Le Rigaud, #0.04, 425 rue Sherbrooke est, **Montreal**, Quebec H2L 1J9
(514) 282-5135

Regroupement tourisme jeunesse
4545, av Pierre-de-Coubertin, **Montreal**, Quebec H1V 3R2
(514) 252-3117 or fax: (514) 252-3119
Ligne sans frais: 1-800-461-8585

Tourisme/Greater Sherbrooke Economic Development Corporation

1308, boul Portland, CP 426, **Sherbrooke**, Quebec J1H 5J7

(819) 822-6195 or fax: (819) 822-6074

Vacances familles inc.

#120, 1291, boul Charest ouest, **Quebec**, PQ G1N 2C9

(418) 682-5464 or fax: (418) 682-0746

Telex: 051-31619

Saskatchewan Tourism Authority

#500, 1900 Alberta St., **Regina**, SK S4P 4L9

306/787-9600; Toll Free: 1-800-667-7191; Fax: 306/787-0715

Tourism Industry Association of Saskatchewan

2154 Airport Drive, **Saskatoon**, Saskatchewan S7L 6M6

(306) 343-3610 or fax: (306) 664-1971

Tourism Regina/Regina Convention & Visitors Bureau

Hwy. 1 East, P.O. Box 3355, **Regina**, Saskatchewan S4P 3H1

(306) 789-8166 or fax: (306) 789-3171

Toll Free: 1-800-661-5099

Tourism Saskatoon

#6, 305 Idylwyld Drive North, **Saskatoon**, Saskatchewan S7L 0Z1

(306) 242-1206 or fax: (306) 242-1955

Toll Free: 1-800-567-2444

Hotels Association of Saskatchewan

1054 Winnipeg Street, **Regina**, Saskatchewan S4R 8P8

(306) 522-1664 or fax: (306) 525-1944

Klondike Visitors Association

P.O. Box 389, **Dawson**, Yukon Territories Y0B 1G0

(403) 993-5575 or fax: (403) 993-6415

Yukon Tourism

P.O. Box 2703, Whitehorse YT Y1A 2C6

403/667-5430; Fax: 403/667-3546

Klondike Visitors Association

P.O. Box 389, **Dawson**, Yukon Territories Y0B 1G0

(403) 993-5575 or fax: (403) 993-6415

Tourism Industry Association of the Yukon

1109 - 1st Avenue, **Whitehorse**, Yukon Territories Y1A 2A9

(403) 668-3331 or fax: (403) 667-7379

Email: tiayukon@knet.yk.ca

American Tourism Associations and Travel Agencies

Alabama Bureau of Tourism and Travel

P.O. Box 4309 **Montgomery**, Ala. 36103

(334) 242-4169

Alaska Division of Tourism

P.O. Box 110801, **Juneau,** Alaska 99811

(907) 465-2010

Arizona Office of Tourism

1100 West Washington Street, **Phoenix**, Arizona 85007

(800) 842-8257 or (602) 542-8687

Arkansas Tourism Office

1 Capital Mall, **Little Rock**, Arkansas 72201

(501) 682-7777

California Office of Tourism

P.O. Box 9278, **Van Nuys**, California 91409

(800) 862-2543 or (916) 322-2881

Colorado Tourism Board

P.O. Box 38700, **Denver**, Colorado 80238

(800) 265-6723 or (303) 592-5510

Connecticut Department of Economic Development
865 Brook Street, **Rocky Hill**, Connecticut 06067
(860) 270-8080

Delaware Tourism Office
99 Kings Highway, Box 1401, **Dover**, Delaware 19903
(800) 441-8846 or (302) 739-4271

District of Columbia Convention and Visitors Association
1212 New York Avenue NW, **Washington,** DC 20005
(202) 789-7000

Florida Division of Tourism
126 West Van Buren Street, **Tallahassee**, Florida 32399
(850) 487-1462

Georgia Department of Industry and Trade
Box 1776, **Atlanta**, Georgia 30301-1776
(800) 847-4842 or (404) 656-3590

Hawaii Department of Tourism
2270 Kalakaua Avenue, Suite 801, **Honolulu**, Hawaii 96815
(808) 923-1811

Idaho Department of Commerce

700 West State Street, **Boise**, Idaho 83720

(800) 635-7820 or (208) 334-2470

Illinois Bureau of Tourism

100 West Randolph, Suite 3-400, **Chicago**, Illinois 60601

(800) 223-0121 or (312) 814-4732

Indiana Division of Tourism

1 North Capital, Suite 700, **Indianapolis**, Indiana 46204

(317) 232-8860

Iowa Department of Tourism

200 East Grand, **Des Moines**, Iowa 50309

(800) 345-4692 or (515) 242-4705

Kansas Travel and Tourism Division

400 Southwest Eight Street, Fifth floor, **Topeka**, Kansas 66603

(800) 252-6727 or (913) 296-2009

Kentucky Department of Travel Development

2200 Capital Plaza Tower, **Frankfort**, Kentucky 40601

(800) 225-8747 or (502) 564-4930

Louisiana Office of Tourism

P.O. Box 94291, L.O.T., **Baton Rouge**, Louisiana 70804

(800) 334-8626 or (504) 342-8119

Maine Office of Tourism

189 State House Station 59, **Augusta**, Maine 04333

(207) 287-5711

Maryland Office of Tourism Development

217 East Redwood Street, **Baltimore**, Maryland 21202

 (410) 767-3400

Massachusetts Office of Travel and Tourism

100 Cambridge Street, Thirteenth Floor, **Boston**, Mass., 02202

(800) 447-6277 or (617) 727-3201

Michigan Travel Bureau

P.O. Box 30226, **Lansing**, Michigan 48909

(517) 373-0670 or 888-784-7328

Minnesota Office of Tourism

375 Jackson Street, 250 Skyway Level, **St. Paul**, Minnesota 55101

(612) 296-5029

Mississippi Department of Tourism

P.O. Box 22825, **Jackson**, Mississippi 39205

(601) 359-3297 or (800) 927-6378

Missouri Division of Tourism

P.O. Box 1055, **Jefferson City**, Missouri 65102

(800) 877-1234 or (314) 751-4133

Montana Department of Tourism

Room 259, **Deer Lodge**, Montana 59722

(800) 541-1447 or (406) 444-2654

Nebraska Division of Travel and Tourism

301 Centennial Mall South, Room 88937, **Lincoln**, Nebraska 68509

(800) 228-4307 or (402) 471-3796

Nevada Commission of Tourism

Carson City, Nevada 89710

(800) 638-2328 or (702) 687-4322

New Hampshire Office of Travel and Tourism Development

P.O. Box 856, **Concord**, New Hampshire 03301

(603) 271-2343

New Jersey Division of Travel and Tourism

20 West State Street, C.N. 826, **Trenton**, New Jersey 08625

(609) 292-2470

New Mexico Tourism and Travel Division

P.O. Box 20003, **Santa Fe**, New Mexico 87503

(800) 545-2040

New York State Department of Economic Development

1 Commerce Plaza, **Albany**, New York 12245

(518) 474-4116

North Carolina Division of Travel and Tourism

430 North Salisbury Street, **Raleigh**, North Carolina 27603

(800) 847-4862 or (919) 733-4171

North Dakota Parks and Tourism Department

Capitol Grounds, **Bismarck**, North Dakota 58505

(800) 435-5663 or (701) 224-2525

Ohio Division of Travel and Tourism

P.O. Box 1001, **Columbus**, Ohio 43266

(800) 282-5393 or (614) 466-8844

Oklahoma Tourism and Recreation Department

500 Will Rogers Building, **Oklahoma City**, Oklahoma 73105

(800) 652-6552 or (405) 521-3981

Oregon Tourism Division

775 Summer Street N.E., **Salem**, Oregon 97310

(800) 547-7842 or (503) 373-1270

Pennsylvania Office of Travel Marketing

P.O. Box 61, **Warrendale**, Pennsylvania 15086

(800) 847-4872 or (717) 787-5453

Rhode Island Tourism Division

7 Jackson Walkway, **Providence**, Rhode Island 02903

(401) 222-2601

South Carolina Division of Tourism

P.O. Box 71, Room 902, **Columbia**, South Carolina 29202

(800) 346-3634 or (803) 734-0122

South Dakota Department of Tourism

711 East Wells Avenue, **Pierre**, South Dakota 5750

(800) S. DAKOTA or (605) 773-3301

Tennessee Department of Tourism Development

P.O. Box 23170, **Nashville**, Tennessee 37202

Texas Department of Commerce, Tourism Division

P.O. Box 12728, **Austin**, Texas 78711

(800) 888-8839 or (512) 462-9191

Utah Travel Council

Council Hall, Capitol Hill, **Salt Lake City**, Utah 84114

(801) 538-1030

Vermont Travel Division

134 State Street, **Montpelier**, Vermont 05602

(800) VERMONT or (802) 828-3236

Virginia Division of Tourism

1021 East Cary Street, **Richmond**, Virginia 23219

(800) 847-4882 or (804) 786-4484

Washington State Tourism

P.O. Box 42513, **Olympica**, Washington 98504

(800) 544-1800 or (206) 586-2088 or (206) 586-2012

West Virginia Division of Tourism and Parks

1900 Washington Street East, Building 6, **Charleston**, West Virginia, 25305

(800) 225-5982 or (304) 345-2286

Wisconsin Division of Tourism Development

P.O. Box 7606, **Madison**, Wisconsin 53707

(800) 432-8747 or (608) 266-2161

Wyoming Division of Tourism

I-25 at College Drive, **Cheyenne**, Wyoming 82002

(800) 225-5996 or (307) 777-7777

International Tourism Associations and Travel Agencies

The following offices will provide valuable information about their countries, including lodging, exchange rates, maps, important sights, weather, entertainment, and so on.

Australian National Tourist Office

500 Fifth Avenue, Suite 2009, **New York**, NY 10110

(212) 496-1990

500 N. Michigan Avenue, Suite 1950, **Chicago**, IL 60611

(312) 644-5556

3284 Yonge Street, **Toronto**, Ontario M4N 3M7

(416) 322-1031 (c/o Pacesetter Travel)

1010 Quest Rue Sherbrook, Suite 1410 **Montreal**, Quebec H3A 2R7

(514) 849-3709

1847 W. Broadway, **Vancouver** BC V6J 1Y6, Suite 210

734-7725

Brazilian Tourism Office

551 Fifth Avenue, Room 421, **New York** NY 10176

(212) 869-7008

British Tourist Authority

551 Fifth Avenue, 7th floor, **New York** NY 10176

(212) 986-2200

111 Avenue Road, **Toronto**, Ontario M5R 3J8

(416) 925-6326 and (888) 847-4885

Danish Tourist Board

655 Fifth Avenue, **New York**, NY 10017

(212) 949-2333

151 Bloor Street West, Toronto, Ontario M5S 1S4

(416) 962-5661

European Travel Commission

630 Fifth Avenue, Suite 610, **New York**, NY 10111

(212) 307-1200

French Government Tourist Office

446 Madison Avenue, **New York**, NY 10022

(212) 838-7800

1981 McGill College Street, Fourth Floor, **Montreal**, Quebec H3A 2W9

(514) 288-4264

German National Tourist Office

747 Third Avenue, New York, NY 10017

(212)661-7200

175 Bloor Street East, Suite 604, **Toronto**, Ontario M4W 3R8

(416) 968-1570

2 Fundy, Place Bonaventure, **Montreal**, Quebec H5A 1B8

(514) 931-2277

Greek National Tourist Organization

645 Fifth Avenue, **New York**, NY 10022

(212) 421-5777

1300 Bay Street, Toronto, Ontario M5R 3K8

(416) 968-2220

Hong Kong Tourist Association

548 Fifth Avenue, **New York**, NY 10036

(212) 869-5008

9 Temperance Street, Third Floor, **Toronto**, Ontario M5H 1Y6

(416) 366-2389

Irish Tourist Board

757 3rd Avenue, **New York**, NY 10017

(212) 418-0800

160 Bloor Street East, **Toronto**, Ontario M4W 1B9

(416) 929-2777 or (800) 223-6470

Japan National Tourist Information

630 Fifth Avenue, **New York**, NY 10111

(212) 757-5640

165 University Avenue, **Toronto**, Ontario M5H 3B8

(416) 366-7140

Korea National Tourism Corporation

480 University Avenue, **Toronto**, Ontario M5G 1V2

(416) 348-9056

Mexican Government Tourism Office

405 Park Avenue, **New York**, NY 10022

(212) 755-7261

2 Bloor Street West, **Toronto**, Ontario M4W 3E2

(416) 925-0704

Netherlands National Tourist Office

25 Adelaide Street, **Toronto**, Ontario M5C 1Y2

(416) 363-1577

New Zealand Travel Commission

630 Fifth Avenue, Suite 530, **New York**, NY 10111

(212) 832-7420

3284 Yonge Street, **Toronto**, Ontario M4N 3M7 (c/o Pacesetter Travel)

(416) 322-1031

Pacific Asia Travel Association

Telesis Tower, #1000, 1 Montgomery St., **San Francisco**, CA 94104 USA

(415) 986-4646

Spanish National Tourist Office

665 Fifth Avenue, **New York**, NY 10022

(212) 759-8822

2 Bloor Street W., Suite 3402, **Toronto**, Ontario M4W 3E2

(416) 961-3131

Swedish Tourist Board

655 Third Avenue, **New York**, NY 10017

(212) 949-2333

2 Bloor Street West, Toronto, Ontario M4W 3E2

(416) 922-8152

Swiss National Tourist Office

608 Fifth Avenue, **New York**, NY 10020

(212) 757-5944

Tahitian Tourist Board

12233 Olympic Boulevard, **Los Angeles**, CA 90064

(213) 337-1040

Taiwan Visitors Association

1 World Trade Center, **New York**, NY 10048

(212) 466-0691

1800 McGill College, **Montreal**, Quebec H3A 3J6

(514) 844-8909

Thailand Tourism Authority

3440 Wilshire Boulevard, **Los Angeles**, CA 90010

(213) 382-2353

5 World Trade Center, Room 3443, **New York**, NY 10048

(212) 432-0433

Trinidad and Tobago Tourist Board

25 West 43rd Street, **New York**, NY 10036

(212) 719-0540

Tunisian Tourist Office

1515 Massachusetts Avenue, NW **Washington**, DC 20005

(202) 862-1850

Turkish Tourism Office

821 United Nations Plaza, **New York**, NY 10017

(212) 687-2194

Venezuelan Tourist Bureau

1 World Trade Center, **New York**, NY 10048

(212) 432-9144

Virgin Islands Tourism Office

1270 Avenue of the Americas, **New York**, NY 10021

(212) 332-2222

Airline Companies in Canada

The following is a list of the head offices for the major airlines operating in Canada. For the Reservations Office of these and all airlines, please refer to 35 McTavish Place NE, Calgary, Alberta T2E 7J7; (403)291-3462 or fax: (403)291-4208

Advance Air Charters

35 McTavish Place NE, Calgary, Alberta T2E 7J7

(403) 291-3462 or fax: (403) 291-4208

Aer Lingus

122 East 42nd St., New York, NY 10168

Toll Free: 1-800-223-6537

Aeroflot, Russian Intn'l Airlines

615, boul de Maisonneuve ouest,

Montreal, Quebec H3A 1L8

(514)288-2125 or fax (514)288-5973

Aerolineas Argentinas

#802, 1235 Bay Street,

Toronto, Ontario M5R 3K4

Toll Free: 1-800-688-0008

Air Canada

Air Canada Centre, P.O. Box 14000, Stn St-Laurent,

Montreal Quebec H4Y 1H4

(514) 422-5772 or fax: (514) 422-5798

URL: http//www.aircanada.ca

Air Jamaica Ltd.

55 St. Clair Avenue West, Toronto, Ontario M4V 1K6

(416) 927-0081 or fax: (416) 927-1524

Air Liberte

1125, boul de Maisonneuve ouest, Montreal, Quebec H3A 3B6

(514) 985-2586 or fax: (514) 985-2588

Air Transit

11600, rue Cargo A-1, Mirabel, Quebec J7N 1G9

(514) 476-1011 or fax: (514) 476-0338

Alitalia

2055, rue Peel, Montreal, Quebec H3A 1V8

(514) 842-8241 or fax: (514) 842-5651

American Airlines Inc.

Lester B. Pearson Airport, P.O. Box 6005, Stn Toronto AMF,

Mississauga, Ontario L5P 1B6

(905) 612-7266 or fax: (905) 612-0144

URL: http://www.amrcorp.com

Air Club International

#205, 11905, route Cargo A-3,
Mirabel, Quebec J7N 1H1
(514) 476-3555 or fax: (514) 476-9818

Air France

#1510, 2000, rue Mansfield, Montreal, Quebec H3A 3A3
(514) 847-1106 or fax (514) 285-8994

Air India

#908, 390 Bay Street, Toronto, Ontario M5H 2Y2
(416) 865-1030 or fax: (416) 865-0716

Austrian Airlines

17-20, White Stone Expressway, White Stone, NY 11357
Toll Free: 1-800-843-0002

Avianca

(Aerovias Nacionales de Colombia)
#1102, 1 St. Clair Avenue West, Toronto, Ontario M4V 1K6
(416) 969-8817 or fax: (416) 969-9926

British Airways

#100, 4120 Yonge Street, Toronto, Ontario M2P 2B8
(416) 250-0250 or fax: (416) 250-1921

BWIA International Airways

#401, 40 Holly Street, Toronto, Ontario M4S 3C3

(416) 440-0112 or fax: (416) 440-1899

Canada 3000 Airlines Limited

27 Fasken Drive, Toronto, Ontario M9W 1K6

(416) 674-0257 or fax: (416) 674-0256

Canadian Airlines International Ltd.

#2800, 700 - 2 Street SW, Calgary, Alberta T2P 2W2

(403)294-2000 or fax: (403)294-2066

URL: http://www.cdnair.ca

Condor Flugdienst

P.O. Box 66178, Chicago IL 60666

(312) 686-8440

Continental Airlines

#500, 3663 Houston Pkwy, Houston TX 77032

Toll Free: 1-800-231-0856

Cubana

#405, 4 Place Ville-Marie, Montreal, Quebec H3B 2E7

(514) 871-1222 or fax: (514) 871-1227

URL: http://www.baxter.net/csa

Czech Airlines

#1510, 401 Bay Street, Toronto, Ontario M5H 2Y4

(416) 363-3174 or fax: (416) 363-0239

Email: csa@baxter.net

Delta Air Lines Inc.

#110, 3300 Place Cote Vertu ouest, Montreal, Quebec H4P 2B7

(514) 856-7600 or fax: (514) 337-8976

El Al Israel Airlines

555, boul Rene-Levesque ouest, #680, 2000, rue Peel,

Montreal, Quebec H2Z 1B1

(514) 875-8910 or fax: (514) 393-9170

Finnair

#402, 20 York Mills Road,

Toronto, Ontario M2P 2C2

(416) 222-0740 or 1-800-461-8651

Telex: 06524460

http://www.se.finnair.com

Icelandair

#410, 5950 Symphony Woods Road,

Toll Free: 1-800-223-5500

Japan Airlines

#2110, 130 Adelaide Street West,

Toronto, Ontario M5H 3P5

(416)364-7229 or fax (416)364-6107

Toll Free: 1-800-525-3663

KLM Royal Dutch Airlines

#2501, 777 Bay Street, Toronto Ontario M5G 2C8

(416)204-5137 or fax (416)204-5180

Korean Air

55 University Avenue,

Toronto, Ontario M5J 2H7

(416)862-8250 or fax (416)862-2105

LOT - Polish Airlines(

514)844-2674 or fax (514)844-7339

55 University Avenue, Toronto, Ontario M5J 2H7

(416) 862-8250 or fax: (416) 862-2105

Lufthansa German Airlines

55 Yonge Street, 10th Floor, Toronto, Ontario M5E 1J4

(416) 360-3615 or fax: (416) 360-3605

Northern Thunderbird Air Inc.

4245 Hangar Road, Prince George, British Columbia V1N 4M6

(250) 963-9611 or fax: (250) 963-8422

Toll Free: 1-800-963-9611

Northwest Airlines

5101 Northwest Drive St. Paul MN 55111-3034

(612) 726-2111 or 1-800-225-2525

URL: http://www.nwa.com

Olympic Airways

503, 80 Bloor Street West, Toronto, Ontario M5S 2V1

(416) 964-7137 or fax: (416) 920-3686

PIA Pakistan International Airlines

#437, 131 Bloor Street West, Toronto, Ontario M5S 1R1

(416) 926-8747 or fax: (416) 926-0507

Qantas Airways

#1705, 1111 West Georgia Street, Vancouver, British Columbia V6E 4M3

(604) 684-1055 or fax: (604) 684-8617

Toll Free: 1-800-227-4500

Royal Aviation Inc.

#503, 6700, Cote de Liesse, Montreal, Quebec H4T 1E3

(514) 739-7000 or fax: (514) 739-7993

Royal Jordanian

45 St. Clair Avenue West, Toronto, Ontario M4V 1K9

(416) 962-3955 or fax: (416) 960-9162

SABENA Belgian World Airlines

#730, 1001, boul de Maisonneuve ouest,

Montreal, Quebec H3A 3C95501

(514) 845-2165 or fax: (514) 845-1978

Skyservice

Electra Road, P.O. Box 160, Toronto AMF, Ontario L5P 1B1

(905) 677-3300 or fax: (905) 678-5654

Email: keith_levia@skysrvs.com

Swissair

#502, 2 Bloor Street West, Toronto, Ontario M4W 3E2

(416) 960-4290 or fax: (416) 960-4295

TAP - Air Portugal
#1410, 1801, av McGill College, Montreal, Quebec H3A 2N4
(514) 849-6163 or fax: (514) 844-1322
Toll Free: 1-800-361-0699

TimeAir
P.O. Box 423, Lethbridge AB T1J 3Z1
(403)329-0355 or fax (403)327-1229

Trans North Air
Airport Hangar C, Whitehorse Airport,
917 Alaska Highway, Toronto Ontario M9W 1K6
(416) 674-0257 or fax: (416) 674-0256

Trans Provincial Airlines
P.O. Box 280, Prince Rupert, British Columbia V8J 3P6
(250) 627-1341 or fax: (250) 627-8307

United Airlines
#310, 180 Bloor Street West, Toronto, Ontario M5S 2V6
(416) 923-2740 or fax: (416) 923-4853

US Air

#100, 4120 Yonge Street, Toronto, Ontario M2P 2B8

Toll Free: 1-800-428-4322

Varig

(Viacao Aerea Rio-Grandense)

#1108, 77 Bloor Street West, Toronto, Ontario M5S 1M2

(416) 926-9511 or 1-800-468-2744

Viasa

(Venezolana Int'l de Aviacion)

#802, 1235 Bay Street, Toronto, Ontario M5R 3K2

Toll Free: 1-800-468-4272

Toll-Free Numbers for Rental Cars and Hotel/Motels

Car Rental Agencies

Avis	800-331-1212
Budget	800-527-0700
Hertz	800-654-3131
National	800-CAR-RENT
Rent-a-Wreck	800-421-7253
Thrifty	800-367-2277
Ugly Duckling	800-THE-DUCK
Value	800-327-2501

International Car Rental Agencies

Auto Europe	800-223-5555
Avis	800-310-2112
Europcar	800-CAR-RENT
Hertz	800-654-3001

Hotels/Motels

Best Western	800-528-1234
Hilton	800-HILTONS
Holiday Inn	800-HOLIDAY
Hotels of the World	800-223-6800
Atlantic City, Reno, Las Vegas, Tahoe Hotels	800-255-5722
Howard Johnson	800-654-2000
Hyatt	800-228-9000
Marriott	800-228-9290
Ramada Inn	800-2-RAMADA
Red Lion	800-547-8010

Toll-Free Airline Numbers

EI	AerLingus	800-223-6537
AM	Aeromexico	800-237-6639
AF	Air France	800-237-2747
AS	Alaska Airlines	800-426-0333
AZ	Alitalia	800-223-5730

AA American Airlines 800-433-7300

BA British Airways 800-247-9297

CO Continental 800-535-0280

DL Delta Airlines 800-221-1212

EA Eastern Airlines 800-EASTERN

JL Japan Airlines 800-424-9235

LH Lufthansa 800-645-3880

NW Northwest

domestic 800-225-2525

international 800-447-4747

QF Quantas 800-227-4500

SA Scandinavian Air 800-221-2350

SR Suissair 800-221-4750

Chapter 3: Reservations

Your next stop -- reservations. This chapter is designed to guide you through the reservation process: what to expect and what to avoid in order to get you to your chosen destination with minimal hassle.

A reservation, or a booking, simply means there is an **intention** by a person to travel on a specific set of dates and flights. That is all. It is not a guarantee that you will actually be on that aircraft. In this imperfect world of ours it is quite possible for a reservation to get "lost" in the computer system or for an agent to "accidentally" erase your file. It is necessary that when you make a booking you get a file number and the name of the agent you spoke with. If, for some reason, your booking cannot be found, at least the airline will have something to work with. If you are not being handled to your satisfaction and/or your reservation cannot be found, ask to speak to a supervisor or a manager. That is what they are there for.

Overbooking is a problem that causes a great deal of inconvenience for the passenger, the airline, and the sales agent, but it is an everyday function of any airline. To my knowledge, there isn't an airline in the world that does not allow either some, or all, of their flights to be overbooked. The term "over-booking" refers to the airline allowing the flight to be booked to a certain number that is over and above the actual number of seats on the plane. For example, an aircraft having one hundred seats may have one hundred and twenty people booked on it. Why? You ask. Because there are countless people who make a reservation, even pay for the ticket, and then decide not to travel, but don't cancel their reservation. So, you have an airplane that appears to be full to capacity when, in fact, it could depart with twenty available seats. This causes disappointment to the twenty people that were turned away believing that the flight was booked to capacity.

The biggest problem with this "overbooking" practice is when all one hundred and twenty people show up at the airport expecting to get on the flight they were booked for. Obviously, twenty people will not be travelling on that flight. Therefore, the time you check in at the airport becomes very important; the first one hundred passengers to show up at the airport and check-in will be the ones travelling. It has nothing to do with when you booked or paid for your ticket. It is simply first come, first serve. "But I made my reservation two months ago," you might say. True enough. However, even if you had made reservations month in advance, a booking or reservation only secures a lower fare, it does not guarantee an actual seat.

Have you ever been at the departure gate area and heard the agent over the loudspeaker asking if anyone would be willing to give up their seat and travel on the next flight in exchange for cash or a travel voucher? This means there is someone at the gate who has a ticket for that flight, but has no seat. At that point the sales agent should be asking for volunteers to deplane in order to get you on board. If they still can't get you a seat, then they should be getting you to your destination as quickly as possible and offering compensation according to company guidelines.

Fortunately, it is not the norm for everyone booked on a flight to actually show up. Also, the sales agent is usually able to get someone to give up their seat. For the few times it does happen, though, it is a very difficult and stressful situation for all concerned.

Believe me when I say my sympathy is with the passenger. I try to imagine how I would feel if I bought theatre tickets two months in advance and upon arriving at the theatre I was told there was someone already in my seat, but that I will be compensated and given a seat for the next performance. My reaction would be, "I don't want to go to the next performance. I want to be at **this** performance!"

The truth is, overbooking is a common practice that is here to stay, so how do you get around it? There are two ways to achieve this. One, whenever you make a reservation try to pre-reserve seats on board the aircraft. Most airlines will allow this, especially if you are travelling with small children, if you are extremely tall, if you have special medical requirements, if you are blind, if you need a wheelchair, or if you are elderly.

If the airline does not have a pre-reserve seat policy, then the only other recourse is to make sure you are at the airport early, approximately one to one-and-a-half hours before departure time. (When it is a special time of year, like Christmas or Spring Break, or if you have to go through Customs, you will have to check in approximately two hours before departure time.)

If you decide to give up your seat for someone else, or if you are forced to accept compensation, you will usually be offered a set amount of cash, (one hundred dollars, for example). Or, you could also be offered double the cash value in the form of a future ticket. (In this example the voucher would be worth two hundred dollars.) Which one would you choose? Unless you have a definite trip planned in the near future, take the cash. It may seem like you are getting less, but you are not. Airlines promote taking the voucher because statistics show that most people do not use the voucher either because of personal commitments, or because it ends up getting lost or forgotten. In this case, your inconvenience ends up costing the airline nothing.

Airline compensation varies and can also include meal and hotel vouchers, free movie and headset, vouchers for bar service, or an upgrade in the class of service. Find out what you are entitled to before you buy your ticket, in the event that you are "bumped" off a flight and, if possible, travel with the airline that will give you the best deal.

TRAVEL CHECK

Remember these reservation tips:

√   get a file number and agent's name when booking

√   check in early to ensure your seat

√   compensation for being inconvenienced -- take cash!

PREPARING FOR YOUR TRIP
Chapter 4: Baggage

Once you have your reservation made the next step is to pack your bags in preparation for your journey. But in order to pack your bags you need to know a few essential facts. How much baggage can I bring on my trip? What will the airline accept? What will I not be allowed to travel with? and How much will it cost me? These are some of the questions I will try and answer in this section.

Don't expect the airline to accept, without charge, all that you want to take with you or bring back home with you. The baggage compartment of an airplane has only so much room for luggage and the rest of the space is set aside for cargo, animals, mail, or important medical supplies. If you want your luggage to travel on the same flight with you, but you don't want to be charged an additional fee, ask your agent what you can and can not take to avoid unpleasant surprises at the airport.

Within North America and on most major airlines, passengers are allowed two pieces of luggage with a maximum weight of seventy pounds per piece. This **does not** mean a total of one hundred and forty pounds. Each bag is considered separate. If you have one bag weighing forty pounds and the second bag weighing one hundred pounds, you will more than likely be charged an excess baggage fee for the second bag. In addition, you are also allowed a bag to take on board the aircraft with you. It must be able to fit under the seat in front of you or in the baggage compartment above your head. Also, if you plan to store it overhead, it must be of a reasonable weight. Expecting to put a forty pound bag in the overhead compartment will only bring you disappointment. These compartments are not designed to hold heavy pieces and with the movement of the aircraft and possible turbulence, it would be unwise to have something that heavy overhead. The general dimensions of the space underneath the seat in front of you are 9"x16"x20." When in doubt measure your carry-on bag before leaving for the airport.

In addition to your carry-on bag, you are allowed a briefcase, a purse, a small bag or any other small personal item, such as a laptop computer. However, if you have a modem you can not use it during take-off or landing as it interferes with cockpit signals. The same policy applies to cellular phones for the same reason. If you are taking a garment bag on board make sure it is not overstuffed with a weeks worth of clothes and shoes. Most aircraft do not have the extra space to accommodate oversized garment bags and you will only cause problems for yourself and the flight crew. I constantly saw business people trying to take these enormous, overstuffed garment bags on board and almost always they were forced to check them in with the rest of the baggage. I know waiting at the arrivals area for your luggage can be time consuming and annoying, but hopefully by the time you walk to the baggage area your luggage will already be on its way. So save yourself a headache and pack a garment bag with the items it was intended for: a suit or a dress, a pair of shoes, and toiletries.

When it comes to excess baggage charges, Domestic charges differ from International charges. Domestic charges will apply if you are travelling within North America or Inter-Europe; International charges occur when your travels cause you to cross a body of water. For example, Toronto to Miami is Domestic and New York to London England is International. Domestic excess baggage charges are usually a flat rate of twenty-five dollars a piece (for example), while internationally it could be one hundred dollars for the first piece of excess baggage, one hundred and twenty dollars for the second piece, and so on. In addition, there is a maximum weight allowance for excess baggage, usually seventy pounds, so be careful. For example, let's say you have two excess pieces of luggage: one weighing twenty pounds , the other eighty-five pounds. You are travelling on a domestic flight and have been told the rate is twenty-five dollars per excess piece. You get to the airport and are charged twenty-five dollars for the bag weighing twenty pounds. But the bag weighing eighty-five pounds will now cost you fifty dollars: twenty-five dollars because it is an excess piece, and an additional twenty-five because it weighs over seventy pounds. Instead of paying fifty dollars, you are now expected to pay seventy-five!

The maximum weight rule may also differ when travelling internationally. The requirements could range from two pieces of luggage at seventy pounds per piece or forty pounds in total, including carry-on bags. So, make sure you ask the agent making your reservation exactly what you are allowed. Don't assume all airlines will be the same because they are not. You could fly to London England and be allowed two pieces at seventy pounds per piece and then take another trip to an island in the Caribbean and find out that the maximum weight allowed is forty pounds in total! Also, when travelling internationally, find out what each airline on your itinerary requires because they may differ. For example, the airline from Zurich to Basel could have a maximum forty pounds baggage allowance, while the airline to Zurich allows two pieces at seventy pounds per piece. This difference in luggage allowance is essential if your connecting flight from Basel has you destined for Zurich!

In addition to your regular baggage allowance, there is also what is referred to as Special baggage. Special baggage items, which include skis, golf clubs, bicycles, pets, fragile items, hunting rifles, ammunition, wheelchairs, etc., may or may not be allowed on the aircraft depending on your airline's policy concerning these items. In the case of hunting rifles, you may have to demonstrate to airport personnel that the rifle is unloaded. Some airlines also require you to sign a form attesting to this fact. Ammunition, which must be in the original containers, has a maximum limit applied to it.

Cargo is another baggage classification which is defined by any article (or pet) which is not travelling on the same plane with you and is therefore governed by different rates and schedules. You can contact the cargo department directly for any information as a reservation or travel agent will not be able to answer your questions as to flight schedule or cost for cargo items. Surf boards, motorcycles, dishwashers, car engines, truck tires, farm animals, outboard motors, wind-surfers, kayaks, canoes, and snowmobiles are **not** considered to be regular baggage and will more than likely have to go as cargo. Imagine what it is like to be at the check-in counter when a passenger tries to check in with a motorcycle and cannot understand why he/she has to send it as cargo.

In addition to the above mentioned cargo items, there are some items that are considered dangerous goods and so are never, ever accepted as checked baggage or allowed on board the aircraft. If you want to transport one of the following items, it will have to go as cargo so it can be properly handled and stored in the cargo hold.

Compressed Gases: Camping gas, butane, butane lighter refills, oxygen*, propane, aqua-lung cylinders

Corrosive Materials: Acids, alkalis, wet cell batteries*, rust prevent ing or removing compounds, sulfur dioxide solution

Etiologic Agents: Chemical kits with agents for human diseases, e.g. vaccine cultures

Explosives: Munitions fireworks, signal flares, sparklers

Inflammable: Petroleum spirits, enamel paint, lacquer

Poisons: Arsenic, cyanides, insecticides, weedkillers

Radioactive Material: Radium, plutonium, polonium, mercury

*Exceptions: **Oxygen** when used for medical reasons and needed on board the aircraft can be carried with the approval of the passenger's doctor and the airline.

Wet Cell Batteries for motorized wheelchairs can be accepted with the approval of the airline with certain conditions. The battery must be removed from the vehicle and packaged properly so as to avoid spillage of battery acid. (Check to see if the airline you are travelling with will do the packaging for you.)

Gasoline power Implements will only be accepted if the gas tank is brand new and has never been used. Used gas anks that have been washed and drained can still retain fuel and are not worth the risk of transporting as regular baggage.

The above list is published by I.A.T.A. (International Air Transportation Association) under Dangerous Goods Regulations and must be adhered to by the airline without exception. Also, any airline can decide to reject any article they feel is dangerous, even if it is not included in the above list. This precaution is for the comfort and safety of all passengers and crew and is not meant as an inconvenience. Some regulations might give the traveller the impression that the airline is overreacting, but there are good reasons for rejecting a particular item. (For more information check the front of your airline ticket.)

There are certain items that are allowed to be included with your check-in baggage, but could be refused to be taken on board with your carry-on luggage. They may seem insignificant to the passenger, but could be deemed dangerous to the person carrying the item or to the people around them should there be an emergency during your flight.   If you are asked to check in one of the following items with your baggage, please realize that someone is looking out for your safety and welfare.

- Knives (all Types)
- Knitting needles
- Toy guns (Some are very realistic looking.)
- Slats of wood or metal
- Glass
- Large picture frames (They can't be stored properly.)
- Scissors
- Irons
- Radios (The signal interferes with the cockpit.)
- Cellular phones (same as above, especially during take-off and landing)
- Darts
- Disposable hypodermic needles
- Straight edge razors

Animals are considered cargo and, believe it or not, the airline is doing you a favor by accepting them as baggage, even if you are being charged a nominal fee. Pets are almost always carried upon paying an excess baggage fee, regardless of how many bags you are checking in.   However, if you are travelling with a charter company check to see if they accept pets because many of them don't. The positive aspect to travelling with your pet is that your pet will travel on the same flight as you and the fee will be considerably lower than regular cargo rates.

An airline's definition of pets is thus: a dog, a cat, or other small animals such as rabbits, hamsters, and some birds. Don't expect to check in at the airport with a goat, a snake, or a chicken. You will only be sent to the cargo department. This may seem like an obvious point but it is well worth mentioning. I remember one such case when a woman going to an agricultural exhibition brought her two hundred and fifty pound Ram to the check-in counter expecting us to accept it. Unfortunately, we had to send her over to the cargo department which is located in another building. In this case, the passenger was greatly inconvenienced. Another time a colleague of mine was confronted with a woman who was travelling with a Boa Constrictor in a gym bag that she intended to check in as regular baggage. By the time she was sent on to her gate she was quite unhappy. She had to buy a pet kennel from us to put the snake in, and she was charged an excess baggage fee. (The snake normally would go as cargo but with the supervisor's approval the snake was cleared as regular pet baggage.)

A few airlines will allow small pets to be taken on board the aircraft but they must be in a leak-proof cage that can fit under the seat in front of you. These leak-proof containers must close properly and lock. Cardboard boxes are not acceptable "cages," neither are gym bags. Since there are a maximum number of pets allowed inside the cabin, mention your intentions at the time you make your reservation. Pet cages can be bought at any pet store and a few airlines sell their own style of cages as well. If the airline sells their own cages, they will usually be cheaper than those at a pet store. Also, a word of caution, if you buy your cage at a pet store and you plan on taking your pet on board, make sure you measure the size of the kennel before you buy it. Many of them are too high to fit under the seat in front of you and, therefore, you will end up having to buy another cage at the airport, or you will have to check your pet in with your other baggage.

If you decide to check your pet in as baggage don't worry about its welfare. It will be in a special compartment of the cargo hold that is heated and pressurized.

Tranquillizing your pet will be up to you and your veterinarian to decide. You are responsible for any medication, food, or water that your pet requires. If you will be tranquillizing your pet the doctor will probably advise you not to give food or water to the animal within so many hours before your flight. Some animals tend to throw up with the combination of pills, food, water, and the altitude.

If you decide to bring your pet on your trip you may find the following list I've compiled, a sort of baggage checklist, useful in preparing for your trip: Proper identification (name and address tag), Certification of good health signed by your veterinarian, Proof of up to date immunizations, pet carrier, pet toys, blanket, first aid kit (including tranquillizers), food (can opener, if needed), thermos of water, plastic bowls, leash and muzzle, flea powder or flea collar, and grooming tools.

There are a lot to things to consider when packing for your trip but remember the rule of thumb - if you don't need it during your flight, check it in with the rest of your baggage. An airline is only required to accept the passenger and personal luggage of that person. Anything beyond a suitcase is open to interpretation and could be rejected. When in doubt, ask.

Upon returning to Canada, The Canadian Food Inspection Agency (formerly Agriculture Canada) imposes a fee of $32.10 for a dog or cat arriving from all international destinations. United States is excluded. If you are travelling with more than one dog or cat, $5.00 will be charged for each additional pet. A proper vaccination certificate must be presented each time. For fee schedules and restrictions to enter pets into other countries, please check with the consulate of the country you will be visiting, or ask the travel agent.

TRAVEL CHECK

Don't carry around all that baggage, remember these tips:

√ international and domestic weight restrictions may differ

√ what you can bring on board - carry-on bag + purse/briefcase

√ dangerous goods have to go as cargo

√ keep others' welfare in mind - check the list for items vetoed

√ pets can travel with you - get the whole scoop from your airline

√ pack properly for your pet - check the list

Chapter 5: Packing

Now that you understand baggage requirements and restrictions it is time to take care of the details. The following lists will help you when packing for your trip. What to pack in your first aid kit (a must for any traveller), what valuable pieces of information and items you should carry on you at all times (a.k.a. Things to Pack II), and a must-do list to ready you for your time away from home. Of course, what to pack in terms of clothing is left up to the individual traveller as the items to be packed will be determined by the climate you are travelling to. If climate is a key issue in helping you choose a travel destination, the temperature conversion chart of Fahrenheit/Celsuis scales and some temperature charts for the most popular vacation sites both within and outside North America may be useful in helping you pack.

For further assistance you may want to check out Appendix B. This section will give you information holidays throughout the world. If you travel to Ontario in October you may accidently find yourself in the middle of Oktoberfest, and there you are -- without your lederhosen! Read this list and you can pull whatever you need out of your suitcase for just the right occasion.

Travellers' First-Aid Kit
- Antiseptic lotion or ointment
- Aspirin or acetaminophen
- Cold and cough remedies
- Gauze bandages and adhesive tape

- Elastic bandages
- Heating pad
- Ice pack
- Identification bracelet
- Insect repellent and insect bite medication
- Medical information regarding condition, allergies, medications, blood type and special needs
- Physician's name, address, phone number
- Prescription medications and refills
- Sunscreen and sunburn relief lotion
- Telephone numbers of emergency contacts
- Thermometer
- Throat lozenges
- Vitamins

Things to Pack II

- Airline or other tickets and travel documents
- Passport, visas, and health certificates
- Medical information and doctor's name and telephone number
- Special prescriptions and/or medications
- Insurance papers
- Credit cards
- Travellers' cheques/personal cheques
- Cash, including some in the currency of the country you are travelling to
- Names/addresses of people to contact in an emergency

- Name/addresses/phone numbers/reservations/numbers and dates for the place you will be staying
- Addresses of friends and family to send mail to

Travellers' Checklist
Things to Do:

- Arrange for the post office to hold your mail or have someone collect it daily
- Stop all deliveries to your home
- Arrange for the care of animals, plants, and lawn
- Put valuables in a safety deposit box
- Notify neighbors/police of absence and let them know how you can be reached
- Leave a key with a neighbor
- Arrange for travellers' insurance
- Reconfirm your airline ticket and other reservations
- Tag your luggage with brightly colored stickers/ribbons for easy identification
- Empty refrigerator and turn it to low
- Turn off hot water
- Lock all doors and windows

Temperatures

C	F	C	F
0	32.0	21	69.8
1	33.8	22	71.6
2	35.6	23	73.4
3	37.4	24	75.2
4	39.2	25	77.0
5	41.2	26	78.8
6	42.8	27	80.6
7	44.6	28	82.4
8	46.6	29	84.2
9	48.2	30	86.0
10	50.0	31	87.8
11	51.8	32	89.6
12	53.6	33	91.4
13	55.4	34	93.2
14	57.2	35	95.0
15	59.0	36	96.8
16	60.8	37	98.6
17	62.6	38	100.4
18	64.4	39	102.2
19	66.2	40	104.0
20	68.0	41	105.8

Some Average Temperatures (F) - North America

Location	Jan/Mar H/L	Apr/Jun H/L	Jul/Sep H/L	Oct/Dec H/L
Acapulco	88/72	90/77	90/75	90/72
Bermuda	68/57	81/59	85/72	79/60
Boston	43/20	75/38	80/55	62/25
Chicago	43/18	75/40	81/58	88/23
Dallas	67/36	90/55	94/68	78/38
Detroit	42/19	77/37	82/55	60/24
Honolulu	77/67	81/68	83/73	82/69
Houston	72/44	90/60	83/70	81/52
Phoenix	75/39	101/53	104/69	86/40
St. Lucia	84/69	88/71	88/73	87/70
San Diego	64/47	69/53	74/62	71/52
San Juan	80/70	85/72	86/75	85/72
Santa Fe	51/19	78/35	80/49	62/20
Seattle	52/36	69/43	72/52	59/38
Toronto	37/15	73/34	79/51	56/21
Vancouver	53/27	83/44	87/59	67/29
Las Vegas	72/29	99/45	103/57	84/30
Los Angeles	67/46	76/50	82/58	76/47
Mexico City	75/42	78/51	74/53	70/43
Miami	78/61	86/67	88/75	83/62
Nassau	9/64	87/69	89/75	85/67

New Orleans 71/47 88/61   90/73   79/48

New York   45/24 77/42   82/60   69/29

Philadelphia 49/26 80/43   85/60   66/30

Some Average Temperatures (F) - Outside North America

	Jan/Mar	Apr/Jun	Jul/Sep	Oct/Dec
Location	H/L	H/L	H/L	H/L
Athens	60/44	86/52	92/67	75/47
Bangkok	93/68	85/76	90/76	88/68
Berlin	46/26	72/39	75/50	56/29
Bogota	68/48	67/51	66/49	66/49
Cairo	75/47	95/57	96/68	86/50
Calcutta	93/55	97/75	90/78	89/55
Caracas	79/56	81/60	80/61	79/58
Dublin	51/34	65/39	67/48	57/37
Hong Kong	67/55	85/67	87/77	81/59
Java	86/74	87/74	88/73	87/74
Jerusalem	65/41	85/50	87/62	81/45
Istanbul	51/37	77/45	82/61	68/41
Lima	83/66	80/58	68/56	78/58
Lisbon	63/46	77/53	82/62	72/47
London	50/35	69/42	71/52	58/38
Madrid	59/35	80/45	85/57	65/36
Manila	91/69	93/73	88/75	88/70

Munich	48/23	70/38	74/48	56/26
Nairobi	79/54	70/38	74/48	56/26
Panama	90/71	87/74	87/74	87/73
Paris	54/34	73/43	76/53	60/36
Quito	72/46	71/45	73/44	72/45
Rome	59/40	82/50	87/62	71/44
Santiago	85/49	74/37	66/37	83/45
Seoul	47/15	80/41	87/59	67/20

TRAVEL CHECK

Within 24 hours of departure:

√ reconfirm reservations with the airline

√ double check arrangements for mail pick-up, newspapers,
plants, pets, etc.

Chapter 6: Frequently Asked Questions

A compilation of frequently asked questions and their answers will address the most common concerns about all aspects of flying. These questions range from pre-boarding issues to in-flight procedures. This section is designed to ease your (the traveller) fears and prepare you for as stress free a trip as possible.

I've bought a special fare ticket and find out I can't travel after all. Will I get my money back?

Whether you get all, some, or none of your money back will depend on the rules of the ticket: Is there an illness or death involved? Have you paid for your ticket? Have you travelled part way or half way on your ticket?

If you have not paid for your ticket or put down a deposit on your reservation, then there is no penalty. It would just be a matter of cancelling or changing your reservation and paying for the ticket according to the rules of the ticket.

If you have put down a deposit or paid for the ticket in full then the situation becomes a little trickier. Let's say you have paid for the ticket and have to change your reservation for personal reasons. Usually you will be able to do so by paying a fee and any other monies, due to change of season or day of travel.

Some airlines will require that you upgrade to the next lowest fare and pay the difference, while some airlines will not allow any change at all. You would simply lose the money already invested and would have to start all over again. The last two examples are extreme and not very common anymore.

If you are cancelling your reservation due to illness to yourself or the death of someone in your immediate family, then usually with a doctor's note or death certificate all penalties will be waived.

If you have already used part of your ticket and you have to change your return date for personal or medical reasons then, in most cases, there will be a nominal fee charged to rebook for another date.

Is there any reason the airline can refuse to let me board the plane?

Yes. If you have a medical condition that would jeopardize the health and safety of yourself or other passengers you could be refused. Also, if you are intoxicated beyond a reasonable level, you become a safety hazard and can therefore be refused. If you are travelling outside your country of birth and do not have the appropriate documents you could be refused. If you are doing something illegal, like travelling on someone else's ticket, or trying to take an unauthorized pet on board you could be refused.

There is fifteen minutes before I land. Why can't I get another drink?

Within ten to fifteen minutes of a plane's arrival the crew is responsible for having all food and beverages locked and securely stowed away, to avoid possible injury to nearby passengers. During that time they must also ensure that all passengers have their seat belts fastened, that cans, bottles, and cups have been collected, that chair-tables have been raised and locked, and that cabin and aisles are free from any loose items. These precautions are taken in the event that if there is an emergency upon landing there are no articles that can impede passengers from exiting the aircraft safely and quickly.

If you need a drink of soda or water to take medication, or you simply need to calm your nerves, the crew will usually be glad to get you something to drink, but it is a practice they discourage in order to keep other passengers from asking them for a drink and disrupting their safety checks.

How soon before departure time should I be at the airport?

The recommended time is one hour. But if you are travelling on an international flight, a charter flight, or if you are travelling out of a busy airport, if it is a prime time of year, like Christmas or Spring Break, or if you have special personal or medical needs, then you should be at the airport approximately two hours before departure time.

Can I bring food to or from another country?

Foods such as all kinds of meat and fruit, as well as plants, cannot be carried between countries. This policy ensures that unwanted insects or bacteria are not transported across the borders. The exceptions are specifically treated and government approved fruit and plants, such as Florida oranges and cactus from Arizona. But these articles are clearly marked government approved and, therefore, can be transported over the borders.

Canned or boxed food, such as pasta or rice, as well as household items such as soap or shampoo can be transported safely. If you have an item that you are unsure about contact the Agricultural Department for the country you are travelling to. They can tell you for certain whether these items are per-missible.

What documents do I need to travel to and from another Country?

The best document to carry is a passport. There isn't a better proof of birth and citizenship. You will always need to show where you were born and in which country or countries you are a legal citizen. Travelling between Canada and the United States only requires a birth certificate and driver's licence, although that may change in the near future. I recommend using a passport. Some countries such as India, Hungary, and Russia will also require that you have a visa, while countries like Africa and parts of South America also require that you have certain shots against diseases such as Cholera, Diptheria, and Malaria. Check with your travel agent as to the documents and shots you will require.

Can a seeing-eye dog be taken on board the aircraft?

Yes. However, the airline will need to know this information at the time you make your reservations, enabling them to make the proper seat selection for you and your dog. Most airlines will not charge you for this service, but double check with them just to be on the safe side.

What's wrong with having a quick cigarette in an airplane washroom? I'm not smoking around other people.

First, it is illegal on most carriers. Certain governments have deemed smoking on board an aircraft to be a health and safety hazard to other passengers.

Second, because smoking is not permitted, there are no ashtrays or suitable containers on board in which to butt out your cigarette. Unfortunately, this encourages many people to throw a cigarette in the washroom waste basket, starting fires as a result. Also, if you are a non-smoker, it would be extremely unpleasant to go to the lavatory to refresh yourself only to walk into one that is filled with smoke. There isn't proper ventilation to accommodate cigarette smoke.

The plane has been circling the airport waiting to land. Will we run out of fuel?

Airplanes are built with extra fuel storage tanks. This way if a flight is taking longer than anticipated the plane can continue to circle the airport.

Can I bring my own liquor on board the aircraft?

Yes. You can bring your own unopened liquor on board with you, but you are prohibited from drinking it. If you want to drink you will have to purchase the alcohol on board.

It is true that many airlines charge for their liquor, but it is not necessarily to raise revenue. Airlines have discovered that, generally, a passenger will drink more than usual if the alcohol is complimentary. There is nothing worse than a drunk passenger. With the crew controlling the amount of liquor distributed, they can prevent a passenger from getting out of control. Also, with people drinking less, it makes the flight a safer one.

The exceptions to charging for alcohol will usually be found in the airlines' First or Business Class cabins. These cabins accommodate far fewer passengers and due to the high cost of travelling in these cabins, the drinks are complimentary. It would still be against airline policy for a passenger in one of these cabins to bring and drink his/her own liquor on board.

Where is the fuel stored on a plane?

In the wings.

I arrived at the gate just when the doors to the aircraft have closed. Why won't the airline let me board the plane?

Once the door to the aircraft has been closed the pilots fire up the engines to depart. To open the aircraft door could mean that the engines would have to be shut down to let you board. Then, once you have boarded, the pilots start the engines all over again. This could prove very costly in time and money to the aircraft for several reasons. First, an airline is often charged large sums of money for leaving a gate after the scheduled departure time, even if it is only a few minutes. Second, if you are leaving from a busy airport, the pilot is designated a "slot time" or an actual departure time on the runway. Missing this slot time could mean an even further delay that would make arrival time at the destination airport late, thereby causing passengers to miss their connection with other flights. It costs the airline money to reroute these passengers, and it could possibly cost the airline additional funds in meal vouchers, taxis, or hotel rooms. It is the domino effect. Because airline schedules are often calculated to the minute, any delay - even if only by a few minutes - can cause a great deal of financial hardship to the airline and the other passengers on board the aircraft.

What's the difference between excess baggage and cargo?

Excess baggage is any additional baggage, whether it is a suitcase, box, or pet, that is over and above the allotted amount of luggage you are allowed to take with you. Also, these additional pieces of baggage are travelling with the passenger on the same aircraft. Excess baggage will usually have a set weight and fee that can be arranged and paid for right at the check-in counter for the flight you are travelling on.

Cargo items are any type of baggage that are not being accompanied by a passenger. These items could include pets, medical supplies, mail, livestock, furniture, and all sizes of boxes. They also include baggage that a passenger tried to check in with them for a specific flight but due to its size, weight, or contents was not suitable as personal baggage.

Cargo rates and schedules differ from that of excess baggage rates and schedules. Cargo rates are calculated according to the size and weight with additional possible charges due to the contents. There is no maximum. When your cargo item travels will depend on the amount of space available on the next aircraft to that particular destination. This does not necessarily mean it will travel on the next flight. Plus, cargo departments are usually separate and away from the passenger terminal. They are run independent of the sales staff at the check-in counters.

If I am delayed at Customs and Immigration will the plane wait for me?

Not likely. Customs and Immigration are not usually concerned with your flight schedule. Their job is to determine whether or not you should be allowed into their country. That is their primary concern.

An airline, although sympathetic to your plight, cannot delay their other passengers for this reason. Therefore, they will very rarely hold the aircraft for you. If you are travelling on a flight that pre-clears Customs and Immigration in your country of origin, allow ample time for possible snags.

I'm stuck in traffic on the way to the airport. I have to make my flight. I call from my car phone to say I'll be a bit late. Will they hold the plane for me?

Again, not likely. With flight schedules being very tight and because the airline has to be considerate of the other passengers on board, it would not be cost effective to delay the plane for you. Once you do get to the airport, though, the airline will do all that it can to get you to your destination as soon as possible. To minimize the risk of arriving late, you may want to have someone drive you to the airport. Besides the extra time it takes to find parking space, airport terminal parking is very expensive and should be avoided if possible. Taxis are another alternative (they should be booked a few days in advance). You could even try Park `N Fly, if the airport offers it.

If my flight is delayed or cancelled due to weather is the airline obliged to compensate me?

This type of delay or cancellation is generally referred to as an "Act of God' and an airline is not responsible for compensating you directly. The train of thought is that the airline was ready and able to depart, but was delayed due to matters beyond their control.

All is not lost, though. If you connected in from another city and will end up having to spend the night in your connection city some airlines will offer you a complimentary hotel room for the night. The airline will also rebook you for the next available flight out. They can arrange for you to make certain phone calls free of charge. If you are travelling on a fare that has restrictive rules, then as long as you remain travelling with the same carrier the change fees will be waived.

If your flight is delayed or cancelled due to an emergency in your destination city, such as a hurricane, earthquake, or severe winter storm, many airlines will allow you to cancel altogether and get a full refund despite certain restrictions on your ticket.

The point about all these above discussed services is that, if offered, they are optional by the airline and not obligatory.

My flight has been cancelled due to a mechanical problem. What are my rights regarding compensation?

Generally, the airline is responsible for compensating you for lost time and possible lost money. You have the right to be put on the next available flight, rebook for a different day without penalty, cancel your reservation and obtain a full refund. If you have connected in from another city and have to stay overnight, then you have the right to ask for a complementary hotel room. If the delay is considerable (for example, a few hours), but you will still travel the same day, then you have the right to ask for a meal voucher while you wait. You have the right to ask the airline to contact a person or persons at your destination airport that can no longer be contacted by phone.

Basically, it is up to the airline to be accountable to the passenger and make the delay as comfortable for him/her as possible. If you are not handled in a reasonable and satisfactory manner, then you should write to the president of the airline for further compensation and if that fails, you may want to contact a lawyer at a later date to see if you are entitled to any other type of compensation.

Why is it so hard to have someone paged at the airport?

It is generally harder to have someone paged at an airport if you are not at that location and have to call the reservation desk for assistance. It means relaying your message to a reservations sales agent who, in turn, must call the airport on a different telephone line. But it is not impossible. It just means that you won't be able to talk to the airport pager directly. If you are in an airport terminal, look for the courtesy paging phone. Almost all airports have them and it is just a matter of picking up the receiver and talking directly to the person who does the paging.

Regardless of how your message is relayed, having someone paged does not guarantee the person being paged will hear his/her name called. For obvious reasons, the volume of a page can only be so loud. It cannot be allowed to interfere with the existing departure and arrival messages. Hearing your name paged above the din can be quite impossible at times. When you are in an airport terminal, do you hear all the messages being broadcast? Not usually. On the positive side, the person concerned will automatically be paged several times.

Why won't an airline tell me if someone is on the flight?

When a passenger purchases an airline ticket it is considered a contract between the traveller and the airline and, therefore, is considered confidential. For security reasons which protect the passenger and airline, that type of information is rarely given out.

Another point that most people don't realize is that a reservation does not mean that a passenger is actually on board an aircraft. Therefore, divulging a person's reservation itinerary is very misleading. The only way to confirm if someone is actually on board an aircraft is to check the flight coupons that are collected when a person boards a plane. After a flight has departed and the sales agents have finished, the coupons are usually sealed and put into a secured area or safe. Those coupons represent cash to the airline and are treated as such and, therefore, will only be opened upon the request of an airline official or the police.

There are many people on board an aircraft that are travelling for highly personal reasons. They could be travelling due to business or political reasons, for personal safety, for sensitive legal reasons, or they could be a celebrity. Whatever the reason, a passenger has the right to privacy and for this reason it is up to the passenger to relay any pertinent travel information. It does not matter whether you are the spouse, boss, good friend, or relative. A passenger's travel information is confidential.

Does the "flying time" consist of only the time spent in the air?

More often than not the published flight time in a schedule or reservations systems will include the amount of time spent on the ground taxiing to and from the gate. I have been on flights, though, where, once in the air, the captain will announce over the loud speaker the actual time spent in the air.

This information is a personal preference of the flight crew, though, and it is not all that common.

The airline has lost or damaged my luggage. What are my rights?

If your baggage has been lost it is up to the airline to try and find your luggage as quickly as possible. They will deliver your luggage to wherever you are staying at no additional cost to you. If there is a delay in finding your suitcases and you are totally without clothes or toiletries, the airline should purchase clothing and necessities for you.

When your baggage has been damaged the airline is responsible for fixing or replacing the luggage and compensating you financially for any articles that have been lost due to the damage. If you are travelling with baggage that is already damaged in some way, you will be asked to sign a damage waiver at the check-in counter.

I've arrived at my destination. What do I do now?

There should be an airline representative meeting the flight to usher you to the baggage area. If there isn't, you will have to look overhead at the baggage area signs and follow the directions. In the baggage area there are usually porters to help with baggage (at roughly $1 per bag, plus tip). If you have to go through customs and immigration there will be an airline representative or customs agent to guide you to the baggage area. Once you pick up your baggage, go outside to the arrivals area to get a taxi or shuttle bus. If you are staying at a hotel have your travel agent determine if there will be a shuttle bus to pick you up. Usually there are bus stops well marked with the hotel's name. Some destinations require you to call the hotel upon arrival so they can pick you up. Other hotels have their buses circle the airport every 15 minutes or so looking for their guests. If you are renting a car you can go to the car rental desk on the arrivals level. It is usually situated close to the baggage area.

Can I fly if I have a cold?

Usually, yes, but you should be aware of a couple of potential problems. With the increased air pressure during landing and takeoff you risk increased pain with clogged sinuses and if you have plugged ears you risk the possibility of damaging or bursting an ear drum, both of which can be extremely painful. If you are really sick and can postpone your trip please do so for your sake and the sake of passengers around you.

I have a ticket, but my reservation has been lost. What happens now?

If you have a valid confirmed ticket for a flight but the reservation has been lost, for whatever reason, the airline has the responsibility of honoring the ticket and securing you a seat on that flight. There could be a problem if the flight is over-sold, you have checked in late, and there are no seats left.

Are there certain items that are best carried on board?

Yes. Any item of value such as money, jewellery, documents, passports, and car and house keys, should be kept with you on board and not checked in with your other baggage. Other items include medication, eye glasses, contact lenses, small fragile items, and liquor in glass bottles.

Can I travel with two infants on my lap?

No. Each row or "bank" of seats has only one extra oxygen mask. In the event of an emergency, someone in that row would be without a mask. So if you are travelling with two infants, you will have to purchase a seat for one of them. If two adults are travelling with two infants it will not be necessary to buy a seat for one of the infants, but the four of you will not be able to sit in the same row.

Is there any way I can avoid jet-lag?

Jet-lag is caused by dehydration due to the combined effect of pressurization and a very low humidity cabin. To counter this effect drink a glass of water for every hour you are in the air. In addition, avoid cigarettes, coffee, tea, and alcohol (contributors to dehydration) while in the air and for a few hours upon arrival. In addition, different time zones can make people feel "off." If you have travelled a great distance try to remain awake until the local night time, going to bed at the same time as the locals. This will help you get your inner clock on the right time zone. Time zones are included in this section to aid you in determining local times in order to help lessen the effects of jet-lag.

Time Zones: North America

(1.30 p.m.)
Newfoundland

Atlantic (1 p.m.): That time which extends farther east of the United States
Halifax, New Brunswick, Prince Edward Island

Eastern (12 noon): That time which corresponds with the eastern United States
ie. Ontario and Quebec
Connecticut, Delaware, District of Columbia, Florida*, Georgia, Indiana*
Kentucky*, Maine, Maryland, Massachusetts, Michigan*, Montreal, New Hampshire, New Jersey, New York, North Carolina, Ohio, Ottawa, Pennsylvania, Quebec, Rhode Island, South Carolina, Tennessee*, Toronto, Vermont, Virginia, West Virginia

Central (11 a.m.)
Alabama, Arkansas, Florida*, Illinois, Indiana*, Iowa, Kansas*, Kentucky*, Louisiana, Michigan*, Minnesota, Mississippi, Missouri, Nebraska*, North Dakota*, Oklahoma, South Dakota*, Tennessee*, Texas*, Winnipeg, Wincousin

Mountain (10 a.m)
Arizona, Calgary, Colorado, Idaho*, Kansas*, Montana, Nebraska*, New Mexico, North Dakota*, Oregon*, South Dakota*, Texas*, Utah, Wyoming

Pacific (9 a.m)
California, Idaho*, Nevada, Oregon*, Vancouver, Washington, Yukon

Allutian (7 a.m.)
Hawaii

Alaskan (8.am.)
Alaska

The Northwest Territories stretch across the Pacific, Mountain, Central, Eastern and Atlantic time zones

*Denotes two time zones

Time Zones: International

The following list gives the time in cities around the world when it is 12 noon, Eastern Standard Time. An (*) indicates the morning of the following day.

Addis Ababa	8 p.m.	Barcelona	5 p.m.
Alexandria	7 p.m.	Beijing	1 a.m.*
Amsterdam	6 p.m.	Belfast	5 p.m.
Athens	7 p.m.	Belgrade	6 p.m.
Baghdad	8 p.m.	Berlin	6 p.m.
Bangkok	12 midnight	Bogota	12 noon

Bombay	10.30 p.m.	Jakarta	12 midnight
Brasilia	2 p.m.	Jerusalem	7 p.m.
Brussels	6 p.m.	Johannesburg	7 p.m.
Bucharest	7 p.m.	Karachi	10 p.m.
Budapest	6 p.m.	Kuala Lumpur	1 a.m.*
Buenos Aires	2 p.m.	Lima	12 noon
Cairo	7 p.m.	Lisbon	5 p.m.
Calcutta	10.30 p.m.	Liverpool	4 p.m.
Cape Town	7 p.m.	London	5 p.m.
Caracas	1 p.m.	Madrid	5 p.m.
Casablanca	5 p.m.	Managua	11 a.m.
Copenhagen	6 p.m.	Manila	1 a.m.*
Delhi	10.30 p.m.	Marseilles	6 p.m.
Dublin	5 p.m.	Mecca	8 p.m.
Edinburgh	5 p.m.	Melbourne	4 a.m.*
Florence	6 p.m.	Mexico City	11 a.m
Frankfurt	6 p.m.	Moscow	8 p.m.
Geneva	6 p.m.	Munich	6 p.m.
Glasgow	5 p.m.	Naples	6 p.m.
Hanoi	1 a.m.*	Oslo	6 p.m.
Havana	12 noon	Panama	12 noon
Helsinki	7 p.m.	Paris	6 p.m.
Ho Chi Minh City	1 a.m.*	Prague	6 p.m.
Hong Kong	1 a.m.*	Rio de Janeiro	2 p.m.
Istanbul	7 p.m.	Riyadh	8 p.m.

Rome	6 p.m.
St. Petersburg	8 p.m.
San Juan	1 p.m.
Santiago	1 p.m.
Seoul	2 a.m.*
Shanghai	1 a.m.*
Stockholm	6 p.m.
Sydney	4 a.m.*
Tangiers	5 p.m.
Teheran	8.30 p.m.
Tel Aviv	7 p.m.
Tokyo	2 a.m.*
Tripoli	7 p.m.
Venice	6 p.m.
Vienna	6 p.m.
Vladivostock	3 a.m.*
Warsaw	6 p.m.
Yokohama	2 a.m.*
Zurich	6 p.m.

EN ROUTE
Chapter 7: Finding Your Way Around the Airport

Here you are -- at the airport. With your bags in tow, head over to the departure level (make sure you were dropped off at the correct terminal or section - some airports are divided into sections i.e. Domestic, Transborder, USA, and International) and head for the check-in counter that your airline operates from. This is where you pick up your ticket (your boarding pass is included in this). If you have special boarding requirements, for example you are accompanied by a seeing eye dog, you are in a wheelchair, or you are an unaccompanied minor this is the time to address these needs with the sales agent so (s)he can make the appropriate arrangements.

Now that you've checked in, picked up your ticket and sent your baggage off, you may find it useful to understand how to read your ticket so you get to where you are going on time and with your sanity intact! I am spending a little time explaining how to read a flight schedule. Fortunately, you will only have to contend with one airline schedule or itinerary. This should lessen the stress immensely.

I have always had a love/hate relationship with airline schedules because although there is a lot of information contained in these booklets, they are sometimes hard to understand or follow. Hopefully you will find this chapter useful, making your next trip that much easier. City codes indicated on the following tickets are "decoded" for you in Appendix A. There you will find a full list of codes and their cities for the most popular destinations.

Destination (to) City

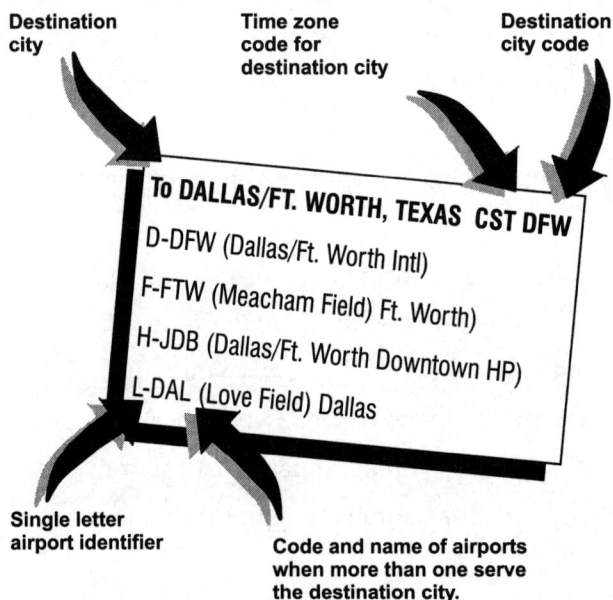

Dallas is a good example of a city that has more than one airport. It is important to check to see which airport you will be using to and from that city, especially if you are making a connection to a different carrier as they could operate out of a different terminal. In addition, your minimum connecting time will also be affected when you are using another terminal. Therefore, if you will be using a different airline ask to see what airport they fly

FLIGHT SCHEDULE

Destination City

Destination
city

Time zone
code for
destination city

Destination
city code

To DALLAS/FT. WORTH, TEXAS CST DFW
D-DFW (Dallas/Ft. Worth Intl)
F-FTW (Meacham Field) Ft. Worth)
H-JDB (Dallas/Ft. Worth Downtown HP)
L-DAL (Love Field) Dallas

Single letter
airport identifier

Code and name of airports
when more than one serve
the destination city.

It might to useful to note here that the more popular the route the more convenient the flight schedule is in terms of connections and departure/arrival times. Check this out with the airline you are travelling with.

Usually there is a representative at the arrival gate to assist with connections. If there isn't, you will have to go to the nearest departure screen to see where your next gate is located. In airports that have more than one terminal, have your travel agent determine if you will need to change terminals and explain to you how to do that, before you pay for your ticket. Usually there are free shuttle buses between terminals that leave for designated bus stops on the arrivals level of the terminal you arrive in.

Direct Flight Schedule

Direct flights are listed from the earliest to the latest departure and all the times are shown as local. Each direct flight is complete on a single line unless an additional information line appears.

DIRECT FLIGHT SCHEDULE

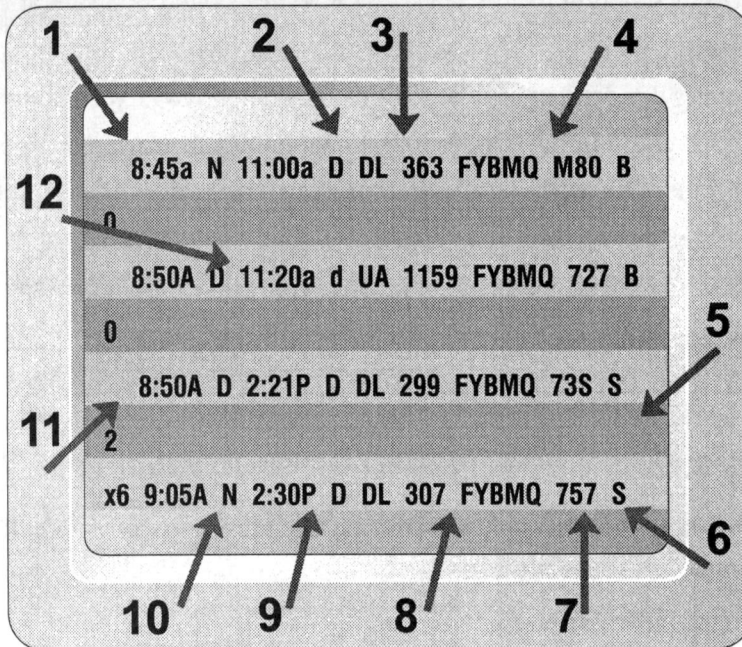

```
    1              2    3              4
   8:45a N 11:00a D DL 363 FYBMQ M80 B
12
  0
   8:50A D 11:20a d UA 1159 FYBMQ 727 B
  0                                       5
   8:50A D 2:21P D DL 299 FYBMQ 73S S
11 2
   x6 9:05A N 2:30P D DL 307 FYBMQ 757 S
                                          6
    10   9    8        7
```

1 - Origin city departure time

2 - Airline code

3 - Flight number

4 - Type of Aircraft

5 - Additional information on this line applies only to the flight above

6 - Number of intermediate stops

7 - Meal Service

8 - Class of service

9 - Destination city single letter airport identifier

10 - Origin city single letter airport identifier

11 - A number (1-7) corresponds to the day of the week the flight operates. Monday (1), Tuesday (2), etc. "X" means **except** and denotes day or days the flight does not operate. No code indicates that the flight operates daily.

12 - Local arrival time

Connecting Flight Schedule

If the direct flights shown are inconvenient for you or if they are unavailable, you may find a connecting flight that suits your needs. Connecting flights are two (single connection) or three (double connection) flights strung together to take you to your destination from your origin city.

Like direct flights, connecting flights are also listed from earliest to latest departure. All the times shown are local times. Read across the lines. In this example, each connecting flight is displayed as a two-line (single) connection. Please bear in mind that in all examples the flights shown are not necessarily valid flights.

In the example of a single connection above, **Originating Flight** TWA (TW) 169 departs Baltimore/Washington Airport (B) at 7:00 a.m. (the departure time is shown in bold face type) and arrives at the **Connecting Point**, St. Louis (STL) at 8:23 a.m. Information on the first line regarding equipment, meals, etc., applies to the Originating Flight.

The second line shows the 9:19 a.m. departure time from the Connecting Point (STL) of connecting flight TWA (TW) 525, arriving at the destination Dallas/Ft. Worth (D) at 11:18 a.m. (The arrival time is shown in bold face type.) The other information on the second line regarding equipment, meals, etc., applies to the connecting flight.

CONNECTING FLIGHT SCHEDULE

Single Connections

```
1        2     3              4

x67 7:00a B 8:23A STL TW 169 FYBQM 72S B 0

    9:19a STL 11:18p    TW 525 FYBQM D9S    0

    9:55a B 11:18a STL TW 245 FYBQM 727 S

0

    11:59a STL 1:50p    TW 551 FYBQM D9S L

0

    9:55a B 11:20a STL TW 245 FYBQM 727 S   5

0
        7        6
```

1 - Destination city arrival time

2 - Airline Code

3 - Class of Service

4 - Type of Aircraft

5 - Connecting city airport code

6 - Connection (E) effective on or (D) discontinued after date shown

7 - A number (1-7) corresponds to the days of the week the flight operates: Monday (1), Tuesday (2), etc.

"X" means **except** and denotes day or days the flight does not operate. No code indicates that the flight operates daily.

Double Connections

A flight schedule for a specific airline will rarely have double connections. Double connections almost always involve another carrier and are only in an airline's flight schedule if the two carriers have formed some sort of partnership or alliance together.

The following ticket is an example of a flight to Allentown from Cozumel via connecting points, Miami (MIA) and Philadelphia (PHL):

CONNECTING FLIGHT SCHEDULE

Double Connections

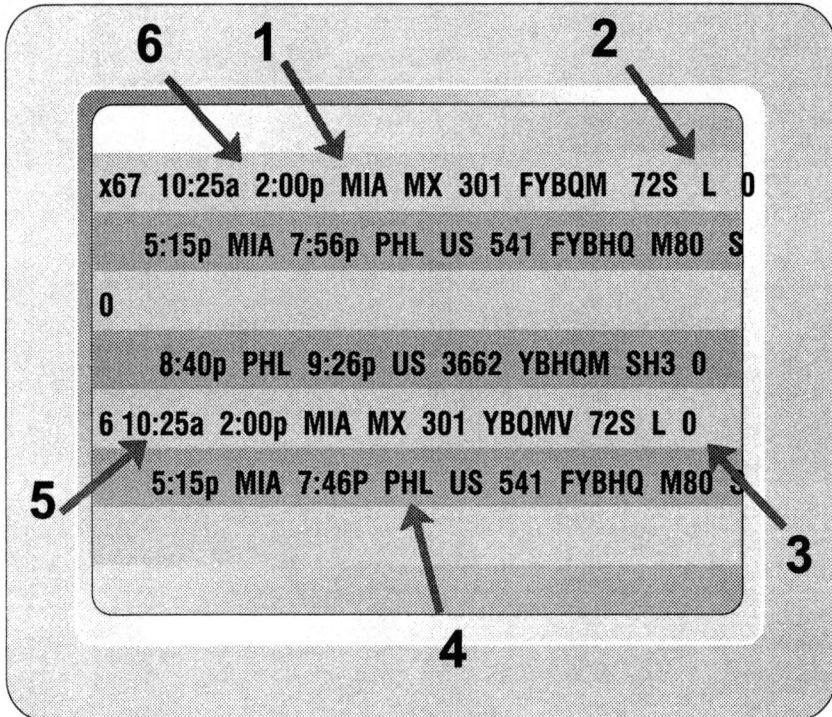

6   **1**   **2**

x67 10:25a 2:00p MIA MX 301 FYBQM 72S L 0

      5:15p MIA 7:56p PHL US 541 FYBHQ M80 S

0

      8:40p PHL 9:26p US 3662 YBHQM SH3 0

6 10:25a 2:00p MIA MX 301 YBQMV 72S L 0

5   5:15p MIA 7:46P PHL US 541 FYBHQ M80 S

                                              3

4

1 - Connecting city airport code

2 - Number of intermediate stops

3 - Meal service code

4 - Flight number

5 - Departure time from connecting city

6 - Arrival time at connecting airport

Chapter 8: Airport Security

To board the aircraft you must have a valid boarding pass with a seat number. Once you go through security at the boarding gate you are cleared to walk on board. If lax security measures in airports is one of your fears, here is a scenario to illustrate just how strict airport security is in order that you, the traveller, will have one less fear to contend with.

Two buddies, Tom and Ryan, were at the airport waiting to go through security to their departure gate. It was a long line-up, filled with business people and vacationers, all intent on their own lives and reasons for travelling on that Friday morning.

Throughout the line could be heard the murmur of voices discussing travel plans, business meetings, and the weather. Some people were en-grossed in their newspapers or magazines, others were still encompassed with sleep and moved with the line automatically, like robots.

Despite the early hour of the day, Tom and Ryan were wide awake and anxious to make it through the line and over to their departure gate as this was their first trip together since they both got married many moons ago.

"I can't believe we are actually getting away, alone, without the wives and kids. We did it buddy!" exclaimed Tom.

"Yeah, I know what you mean. Sun and surf here we come," said Ryan. "I just wish this line would move faster.

The two men succeeded in getting closer to the security wall. The x-ray machines were finally in sight. As they got closer a poster on the wall beside the entrance became more visible and it caught Ryan's eye.

"Hey, Tom. Look at that poster up there about terrorists: `Terrorism is no laughing matter.' I'll say. I've seen some pretty ugly terrorists!" he laughed.

"Hey man, don't make jokes. The sign says you can go to jail for making jokes about terrorism or guns. So shut-up will ya."

"Yeah, right. They're not going to throw you in jail for that. Besides, what's the big deal? We hardly look like the terrorist-type. Lighten up."

They made it to the x-ray machines and Tom handed over his boarding pass to the security guard, emptied his pockets into a bowl and stepped through the x-ray machine.

"Thank you sir," said the security officer and handed Tom back his personal items. Now it was Ryan's turn to go through.

"Sir, will you please empty your pockets into this bowl and step through the x-ray machine?"

With a snicker Ryan responded, " I can't. The bowl is too small."

"What do you mean?"

"My gun's too large to fit in that bowl," he laughed.

With a shocked look on her face, the security guard signalled to two police officers off in the corner and they immediately came up to Ryan and grabbed both his arms taking him away from the line-up.

"Hey, what's going on and where did you two come from?" he shouted.

"Come with us." One of the officers said.

"Why? I didn't do anything."

"You said you have a gun."

"Yeah, but I was only kidding. You can check my pockets and see that I don't have a gun. I'm just going on vacation with my buddy," Ryan pleaded.

"You **were** going on vacation with your buddy. Now you are coming to the police station with us," the officer informed him.

Tom, not realizing all that had transpired and thinking that Ryan was right behind him, turned to see him being taken away by the police. Quickly, he went over to the security officer and asked, "Hey, where are they taking my buddy?"

"He is being taken to the police station in the terminal."

"Why?"

The officer didn't look at Tom right away and continued to check boarding passes in order to process the remaining passengers headed for their gates.

Tom went up closer and shouted, "Why are they taking him away?"

Still, without looking at him, the officer answered, "Because he said he had a gun so I called over the police."

"He was only kidding. You should know that," he screeched.

The officer stopped what she was doing and turned to look at Tom. With a cold stare she replied, "No, I don't know that."

"But if you had checked his pockets you would have seen..."

"Look. Jokes like that are not funny to us and I can't afford to assume anyone is kidding. Maybe your friend will be more careful next time. Now more along and let me get on with my job."

"Oh, for God's sake!" Tom exclaimed. He then ran out towards where Ryan had been taken by the police.

Ryan was grilled for several hours. His baggage was removed from the plane, which delayed the departure of the flight, and the police went over his personal belongings with a fine tooth comb. Once satisfied that he was only "joking" about the gun, he was severely reprimanded, fined, and then released.

Having missed their flight and not being able to get their money back on their tickets or rebook for another day, the two men went home dejected. But none of that was going to compare to the upcoming embarrassment of having to face their wives and friends and explain what happened.

Airline personnel and security staff never think it is funny when there is a joke made about terrorism or weapons. They can't afford to. Every remark or intonation about a threat to the security and safety of an airplane has to be treated as genuine. You may think it is funny, but it isn't. So save your jokes for subject matter that is not so serious.

Chapter 9: In-Flight Safety Procedures

Flying can be a traumatic experience even though you get to your destination faster than by any other mode of transportation. Statistics on the safety of flying do not help to ease fears when there is an accident, or you are on board and the plane is caught in a sudden air pocket and drops several hundred feet in just a few seconds. But through knowledge comes wisdom. So hopefully, this chapter in which I explain staff expertise and in-flight procedures will help ease some of your anxieties about flying.

Airplanes, especially commercial airplanes, have always been a source of fascination to me. How can so much weight get off the ground in the first place? In all my years working at the airport I never stopped being amazed that a 747, with five hundred people on board, could make it into the air, but they always did and not because of luck. They made it airborne because of remarkable engineering and technology, not to mention the years of training and skill that the pilots possess.

We all know that the pilots are highly trained. Those men and women in the cockpit have spent thousands of hours and many years training in order to get behind those controls. An airline won't hire just anybody; these pilots are the best of the best and they are flying with the finest technology. But what about the rest of the crew? We'll start our discussion about the crew by taking a look at the flight attendants.

What type of safety training do flight attendants have? They have to know how to assist with all kinds of emergency, everything from airsickness to a plane crash. They know everything about the aircraft they serve on:

everything from the exit doors, to oxygen, life jackets, and preparing for crash
landing on the ground or on water. They know where every piece of equipment is on that plane and they know how to use it quickly and efficiently.
They know how to function in the event of fire or smoke. They know how
to evacuate a plane in under three minutes should it land on the water. They
know about pressurization, turbulence, and air pockets. They also know how
to prepare passengers for an emergency landing. Most airlines have 16 week
training programs which include all of the above mentioned procedures.

With the many advances in customer service it is easy to look upon your
crew as merely "waiters" and "waitresses," but their primary function fo-
cuses on the safety of the passengers on board in the event of an emergency.
Fortunately, their safety training and skills aren't needed too often and then
they concentrate on serving drinks and meals. Sure, they can serve drinks
and meals, provide pillows and blankets, work in a kitchen the size of a
bathroom, manoeuvre a meal cart down an aisle the width of their hips, and
administer the finer points of service, but that is a sideline for them. Their
primary function is your safety. Period. These men and women spend
weeks training and are not allowed to fail any of their exams. They end up
knowing almost as much about the aircraft as the pilots.

I once heard someone say that only the people "willing" to survive an air
crash, do. It seems like a strange thing to say. After all, doesn't everyone
want to survive a crash? However, the person went on to say that only in
preparing for a disaster do you stand a chance of surviving.

Let me be more specific. In an emergency the people that have watched
a safety demonstration before takeoff, have read the safety card on the air-

craft, have noted the nearest emergency exit, and those people who always keep their seat belt loosely fastened during the entire flight tend to have a better chance of survival than the ones that do not do these things. Also, what you wear can be important. How? In the event of a fire, synthetic clothing can melt into the skin and can cause severe burns. Clothing made of cotton or wool is best to wear and is usually more comfortable to travel in anyway. These safety precautions do not guarantee your survival but they greatly increase your chances of avoiding substantial injury.

I used to get asked this question a lot by passengers: "Where is the safest place to sit on an airplane?" The running joke was, "over the flight recorder," because the "black box" always survives a crash. But, in truth, there isn't one place that is safer than the rest. It all depends on the type of emergency that occurs and if the plane has to land suddenly. Unfortunately, only then, will anyone know what was the better seat to be in. Odds are that you will be like the majority of passengers and never have to worry about severe turbulence, let alone an emergency landing. So sit back, with your seat belt fastened, and enjoy your flight.

Turbulence is something that can happen at any time and with no warning. Most of the time the captain will be able to warn passengers and crew ahead of time, but sometimes that is not possible. Everything can be smooth and calm and suddenly the airplane hits an air pocket causing the plane to drop a hundred feet. If you do not have your seat belt fastened you could get lifted or thrown from your seat and suffer injuries. That is why you should always have your seat belt loosely fastened when seated.

Once, I was seated beside a very nervous flier when the plane encountered some mild turbulence. The woman looked around with fright and when she saw that the overhead baggage compartments and chair-backs were also jiggling, she became afraid that the plane was falling apart! The truth is an aircraft is built with some "give" to allow the plane to move with turbulence. If the plane was rigid, it could develop cracks. So try to relax and ride it out. It usually won't last more than a few seconds and all will be calm again. I usually bring along my Walkman, a few relaxation tapes, and a good book so that if the flight becomes a little rough I have something to calm myself down. Bring something along that works for you and stay away from too much alcohol. Your rate of intoxication increases with the high altitude and can make you more nervous and excited. Plus, if there is an emergency, with your reaction time dulled, you could be a hindrance to your own or someone else's safety.

Travel sickness may be something you have to contend with while in the air. However, most travel sickness can be overcome by taking anti-nausea medicine (for example, Gravol) and pain medication for headaches (Aspirin, for example). Also, drink lots of water, but avoid coffee, tea, and alcohol (all of which can dehydrate you). The crew will also supply you with a pillow and blanket on request. You may also want to remove your shoes (the altitude can swell your feet), get up and walk around once in a while, or get a cold compress from the crew. In addition, if the flight has a smoking section either limit your cigarettes or sit in a non-smoking seat and get up and go to the smoking section went you want a cigarette.

The major cause of the fear of flying is the lack of control that a passenger has over the situation. However, the truth is that you stand a better chance of injury or death while driving your car than you do flying on an airplane. Just think of the thousands of flights that take off from airports around the world every day and compare that with the thousands of cars on the road each day. Statistically speaking, air travel is far safer than any other mode of transportation. So sit back and enjoy your flight.

Chapter 10: Tip Charts and International Measurements

The following few pages will offer you some helpful information when you, as a traveller, find yourself in untrodden territory. Seemingly common-place practices may lead to annoying and sometimes embarrassing situations if you are in unfamiliar territory dealing with unfamiliar customs and prac-tices. It is for just such times that I have included useful information such as measurement units and tipping "tips." I hope this tidbit of information will make your trip that much more enjoyable.

Tipping

Tipping is a way of showing your satisfaction with the service, whether it is with a restaurant, a hotel, or a taxi. Many companies and special serv-ices, such as cruise lines, require certain practices and customs to be fol-lowed. However, tipping can be a common source of confusion and frustra-tion because the traveller is often unsure when, where, and how much to give for services rendered. I have compiled this guideline of tipping amounts for average service to lessen the traveller's frustration. Common rule of thumb which may help: a larger tip than indicated should be reserved for extraordi-nary service. A small tip or no tip at all is given when the service has been poor. The following is intended as a suggested list only.

Restaurant
waiter or waitress   15% of the bill

headwaiter/maitre d'	none, unless special services are provided; then, about $5
wine steward	15% of wine bill
bartender	10-15% of bar bill
busboy	none
counter servers	15% of bill
coat check attendant	$1 per coat
restroom attendant	50 cents
car park attendant	50 cents

Hotel

chambermaid	$1 a night or $5-$10 a week; None for one night
room-service	15% of bill
bellhop	$1 per bag
lobby attendant	$1 for help with luggage or finding a taxi on the street
desk clerk	none; $5 for special service given during long stay

Train

dining car waiter	15% of bill
stewards/bar-car waiter	15% of bar bill
redcaps	$1 per bag

Airport

skycaps	$1 per bag
in-flight staff	none

Cruise Ship

cabin steward	2.5-4% of total fare
dining-room steward, cabin boy	
bath steward, bar/wine steward	5-7.5% of total fare divided among them; paid at the end of each week

Taxi

driver	15% of fare

Barbershop

haircutter	15% of the cost

Beauty shop

one operator	15% of bill to person who sets hair; 10% divided among others
manicurist	$1-$2 or more, depending on cost

Sports Arena

usher	50 cents - $1 per party if shown to your seat

The majority of countries around the world use the Metric System in which units are measured in increments of 10. The British Commonwealth and former countries under British rule still use the Imperial System. Canada was using the Imperial System until the mid 70's, but has since converted all units of measurement to Metric. Included below are conversion factors needed in order to convert from one system of measurement to the other.

Common Measurement Units

Known	To Get	X's By
inches	millimeters	25.4
feet	centimeters	30.0
yards	meters	0.9
miles	kilometers	1.6
millimeters	inches	0.04
centimeters	feet	0.4
meters	yards	1.1
kilometers	miles	0.62
fluid ounces	grams	28.0
pounds	kilograms	0.45
kilograms	pounds	2.2
pints	liters	0.47
quarts	liters	0.95
gallons	liters	3.8
litres	pints	2.1
litres	quarts	1.06
litres	gallons	0.26
grams	fluid ounces	0.035

Chapter 11: Diplomatic and Consular Representatives

Diplomatic & Consular Representatives in Canada

Republic of Albania
Embassy of Albania (to Canada): #1010, 1511 K St. NW., **Washington** DC 20005 202/222-4942; Fax: 202/628-7342 Ambassador, USA & Canada; His Excellency Lublin Dilja

People's Democratic Republic of Algeria
Embassy of Algeria: 435 Daly Ave. **Ottawa** ON KIN 6H3 613/789-8505; Fax: 613/789-1406 Ambassador, His Excellency Abdessiam Bedrane; Counsellor, Economic & Commercial Affairs, Ahmed Bouchentouf

Antigua & Barbuda c/o Organization of the Eastern Caribbean States
Dartmouth: Hon. Consul, Castor Williams, 13 Oathill Cr., Dartmouth NS B2Y 4C3, 902/465-8127; **Toronto:** Consul, Madeline Blackman, #304, 60 St. Clair Ave. East, Toronto ON M4T 1N5, 416/961-3143; Fax: 416/961-7218

Argentine Republic
Embassy of the Argentine Republic: #910, 90 Sparks St., **Ottawa** ON K1P 5B4 613/236-2351; Fax: 613/235-2659; Commercial Office Fax: 613/563-7925; Ambassador, Her Excellency Lillian O'Connell de Alurralde; Minister, Economic & Commercial Affairs, Guillermo Azrak; **Montreal**: Consul General, Oscar Gallié, #710, 2000, rue Peel, Montreal PQ H3A 2W5, 514/

842-6582; Fax: 514/842-5797; Toronto: Consul General, Jorge Vinuela, #5840, 1 First Canadian Place, **Toronto** ON M5X 1K2, 416/955-0232; Fax: 416/955-0868

Commonwealth of Australia

Australia High Commission: #710, 50 O'Connor St., **Ottawa** ON K1P 6L2; 613/236-0841; Fax: 613/236-4376; High Commissioner, His Excellency Frank C. Murray; Deputy High Commissioner, Pat Hardy; Counsellor, Andrew Engel; **Toronto**: Consul General, Ian Taylor, #314, 175 Bloor St. East, Toronto ON M4W 3R8; 416/323-1155; Fax: 416/323-3910; Telex: 06-219762; **Vancouver**: Consul, Graeme South, World Trade Center Office Complex, #602, 999 Canada Place, Vancouver B.C. V6C 3E1; 604/684-1856

Republic of Austria

Embassy of Austria: 445 Wilbrod St., **Ottawa** ON K1N 6M7 613/789-1444; Fax: 613/789-3431; Ambassador, His excellency, Dr. W. Lichem; **Calgary**: Hon. Consul General, Hans Ockermueller, 1131 Kensington Rd. NW, Calgary AB T2N 3P4; 403/283-6526; Fax: 403/283-1512; **Halifax**: Hon. Consul, Michael Novac; #710, 1718 Argyle St. Halifax NS B3J 3N6; 902/429-8200; Fax: 902/425-0581; **Montreal**: Hon. Consul General, Ulrike Billard-Florian, #1030, 1350, rue Sherbrooke Ouest, Montreal PQ H3G 1J1, 514/845-8661; Fax: 514/284-3503; Montreal: Trade Commissioner, Peter Paul Schwartz, #1410, 1010, rue Sherbrooke ouest, Montreal PQ H3A 2R7, 514/849-3708; Fax: 514/849-9577; **Regina**: Hon. Consul, E.F. Anthony Merchant; #100, 2401 Saskatchewan Dr. Plaza, Regina SK S4P 4H9. 306/359-7777; Fax: 306/

522-3299; **Toronto**: Hon. Consul General, Dr. H.G. Abromeit; #1010, 360
Bay St., Toronto ON M5H 2Y6; 416/ 863-0649; Fax: 416/869-7851; Toronto:
(Commercial Affairs), Gerard Müller; #3330, 2 Bloor St. East, Toronto ON
M4W 1A8; 416/967-3348; Fax: 416/967-4101; **Vancouver**: Hon. Consul
General, Graham P. Clarke: #206, 1810 Alberni St., Vancouver BC V6G 1B3;
604/687-3338; Fax: 604/681-3578; Vancouver: Trade Commissioner,
Wolfgang Harwalik, #1380, 200 Granville St. Vancouver BC; V6C 1S4; 604/
683-5808; Fax: 604/662-8528; **Winnipeg**: Hon. Consul. John Klassen, 330
Sault-eaux Cr., Winnipeg MB R3C 3T2; 204/885-2882; Fax: 204/885-7557

Republic of Azerbaijan
Embassy of Azerbaijan (to Canada); #700, 927-15th St. NW, **Washington**
DC 20005; 202/842-0001; Fax: 202/842-0004; Email:
azerbaijan@mcimail.com; Ambassador Designate, His Excellency Hafiz Mir-
Jalal Oglu Pashayev

Commonwealth of the Bahamas
High Commission of the Bahamas; #1020, 360 Albert St. **Ottawa** ON K1R
7X7; 613/232-1724; Fax: 613/232-0097; High Commissioner, His Excellency
Luther E. Smith; Third Secretary, Melvin V. Claridge

State of Bahrain
Embassy of Bahrain (to Canada); 3502 International Dr. NW. **Washington**
DC 20008; 202/342-0741; Fax: 202/362-2192; Ambassador, His Excellency

Mohammed Abdel-Ghalfar; Montreal, Consul. Abdulnabi Mussayab Mohammed: 1869, boul René Lévesque Ouest, Montreal PQ H3H 1R4; 514/931-5988

People's Republic of Bangladesh

Bangladesh High Commission: #302, 275 Bank St., **Ottawa** ON K2P 2L6;
613/236-0138/9; Fax: 613/5673213; High Commissioner, Mufleh R. Osmany

Barbados

High Commission for Barbados: #600, 130 Albert St., **Ottawa** ON K1P
5G4; 613/236-9517; Fax: 613/230-4362; Email: barhcott@travel-net.com;
High Commissioner, Her Excellency June Clarke; First Secretary, Simone
Rudder; **North York**: Consul. General, Errol Humphrey; #1800 5160 Yonge
St., North York, ON M2N 6L9, 416/512-6565; Fax: 416/512-6580; Vancou-
ver: Hon. Consul. Annette Goodridge; #401, 2020 Haro St. Vancouver BC
V6G 1J3; 604/8762-4444; Fax: 604/681-0740; **Westmount:** Consul. Jennifer
V. Barrow, #523, 4800, de Maisoneuve Ouest, Westmount PQ H3Z 1M2; 514/
932-3206; Fax: 514/932-3775

Kingdom of Belgium

80 Elgin St., 4th Fl., **Ottawa** ON K1P 1B7; 613/236-7267; Fax: 613/236-
7882; Telex: 053-3568; Ambassador, His Excellency Christian Fellens; Counsellor, Luc Jacobs; **Calgary**: Hon. Consul, Bernard Callebut, 908-18 Ave. SW
Calgary AB T2P 0H1, 403/265-5777; Fax: 403/244-2094; **Edmonton**: Hon.
Consul, George de Rappard: #107, 4990-92 Avenue, Edmonton AB T6B
2W1, 403/425-0184; Fax: 403/466-2832; **Halifax**: Hon. Consul, Joz de Belie,

P.O. Box 1590, Stn. M. Halifax NS B3J 2Y3, 902/423-6324; **Montreal**: Consul General, Louis Engelen; #850, 999, boul de Maisonneuve Ouest, Montreal, PQ. H3A 3L4, 514/849-7394; Fax: 514/844-3170; Telex: 05-268691. **Toronto**: Consul General, Claude Rijmenans, #2006, 2 Bloor St. West, PO Box 88, Toronto, ON, M4W 3E2, 416/944-1422; Fax: 416/944-1421; Telex: 06-23564 CONSUBEL TOR. **Vancouver**: Hon. Consul. Dirk De Vuyst, 3 Bentall Centre, Vancouver, BC. V7Y 1J5, 604/691-7566; Fax: 604/688-2827. **Winnipeg**: Hon. Consul. Paul Deprez, 15 Acadia Bay, Winnipeg, MB. R3T 3J1, 204/261-1415

Belize
High Commission for Belize: 2535 Massachusetts Ave. NW, Washington, DC 20008. 202/332-9636; Fax: 202/332-6888. High Commissioner, His Excellency Dean Russell Lindo. **Montreal**: Hon. Consul. General, Harry J.F. Bloomfield, Q.C., 1080 Beaver Hall Hill, Montreal PQ. H2Z 1S8. 514/871-4741; Fax: 514/397-0816. **Vancouver**: Consul General, Pamel Suzanne Picon, 904-1112 West Pender St., Vancouver, BC. V6E 2S1, (604) 683-4517; Fax: (604) 683-4518

Republic of Benin
Montreal: Hon. Consul, Pilar Ramos de Arto, 18 av Severn, Montreal PQ H3Y 2C7; 514/989-5132; Fax: 514/989-5177; **Vancouver**: Hon. Consul, Dr. A.S. Andree, 1130, 1040 West Georgia St. Vancouver BC V6E 4H1; 604/685-8120

Republic of Bolivia

Embassy of Bolivia: #504, 130 Albert St., **Ottawa**, ON, KIP 5G4; 613/236-5730; Fax: 613/236-8237; Ambassador, Vacant; Minister-Counsellor & Chargé d'Affaires, a.i., Myriam Paz Cerruto; Edmonton: Consul General, Carlos Pechtel, 11231; Jasper Ave. **Edmonton** AB T5K 0L5; 403/488-1525; Fax: 403/4880350; **Montréal**: Hon. Consul, Pilar Ramos de Arto, 18av Severn, Montréal PQ H3Y 2C7; 514/989-5132; Fax: 514/989-5177; **Vancouver**: Hon. Consul, Dr. A.S. Andree; 1130, 1040 West Georgia St., Vancouver BC V6E 4H1; 604/685-8121; Fax: 604/685-8120

Republic of Botswana

High Commission for Botswana (to Canada): c/o Republic of Botswana; #7M, Intelsat Bldg., 3400 International Dr., NW, **Washington** DC 20008; 202/244-4990; Fax: 202/244-4164; Telex: 64221; Ambassador, His Excellency Botsweletse Kingsley Sebele; **Toronto**: Hon. Consul, Douglas G. Hartle, 14 South Dr., Toronto ON M4W 1R1; 416/ 978-2495; Fax: 416/324-8239

Federative Republic of Brazil

Vacant; Edmonton: Hon. Consul, Peter Elzinga, 8619 Strathearn Dr., **Edmonton** AB T6C 4C6; 403/466-3130; Fax: 403/465-0247; **Halifax**: Hon. Consul, Raymond W. Ferguson, 3630 Kempt Road, P.O. Box 8870 Stn A. Halifax NS B3K 3Y4, 902/455-9638; **Montreal**: Consul General, Antonino Porto E. Santos, #1700, 2000 rue Mansfield, Montreal PQ H3A 3A5, 514/499-0968; Fax: 514/499-9363; **Toronto**: Consul General, Luiz Fernando-Gourea de

Athayde, # 1109, 77 Bloor St. West, Toronto ON M5S 1M2, 416/ 922-2503; Fax 416/ 922-1832; **Vancouver**: Deputy Consul General, Raul Campos de Castro: #1300, 1300 Pender St. West, Vancouver BC V6E 4G1; 604/687-4589; Fax: 604/681-6534

Brunei Darussalam

High Commission of Brunei Darussalam: #400, 30 Metcalfe St. **Ottawa** ON K1P 5L4; 603/234-5656; Fax: 603/234-4397; High Commissioner: Pengirian Abdul Momin; First Secretary: Magdelene Teo Chee Siong

Republic of Bulgaria

Embassy of the republic of Bulgaria: 325 Stewart St., **Ottawa** ON K1N 6K5; 613/789-3215; Fax 613/789-3524; Ambassador, His Excellency Stan Danev; Counsellor and Deputy Head of Mission, Svilen Iliev; Counsellor, Economic & Commercial, Nikolay Babev; **Toronto**: Consul General, Dimitar Filipov Serafimov: #406, 65 Overlea Blvd., Toronto ON M4H 1P1; 416/696-2420; Fax: 416/696-8019

Burkina-Faso

Embassy of Burkina-Faso: 48 Range Road, **Ottawa** ON K1N 8J4; 613/238-4796; Fax: 613/238-3812; Ambassador, Mouhoussine Nacro; Counsellor, Eric Tiare; Magog: Hon. Consul, Pierre Bastien; 1718, ch Alfred-Desroches, RR#2, **Magog** PQ J1X 3W3; 819/847-1747; **Toronto**: Hon. Consul, Peter K. Large, #610, 372 Bay St. Toronto ON M5H 2W9; 416/867-8669

Republic of Burundi

Embassy of Burundi: 50 Kaymar St. Rothwell Heights, **Gloucester** ON K1J 7C7; 613/741-8828; Fax: 613/741-2424; Ambassador, Fredéric Ndayegamiye; Ambassador, Hermenegillde Nkurbagaya; **Montreal**: Hon. Consul, Jean-Guy Laurendeau; 4017 Lacombe St. Montreal PQ H3T 1M7; 514/ 739-5204; **Toronto**: Hon. Consul, David Michael Wright, 5 Dewbourne Ave. Toronto ON M5P 1Z1, 416/932-8212; Fax: 416/922-3667
*Due to political instability in Burundi, the ófficial ambassador to Canada was not known at the time of publishing

Central African Republic

Embassy of Central African Republic (to Canada): 1618-22nd St. NW, **Washington** DC 20008; 202/483-7800; Ambassador, His Excellency Jean-Pierre Sohahong-Kombet; Counsellor, Ndinga Gaba; **Montreal**: Hon. Consul General, Jean-Francois Boisvert; 225 rue St-Jacques St. Ouest, Montreal PQ H2Y 1M6 ; 514/849-8381; **Ottawa**: Hon. Consul, Stuart E. Hendin: 726 50 O'Connor St., Ottawa ON K1P 6L2, 613/563-4804; Fax: 613/563-3878; **Quebec**: Hon. Consul, Marc Dorion, #201, 112 Dalhousie St., Quebec PQ G1K 4C1, 418/692-1532; Fax: 613/563-3878; Quebec PQ G1K 4C1, 418/692-1532; Fax: 418/692-5091

Republic of Chile

Embassy of Chile: #605, 151 Slater St., **Ottawa** ON K1P 5H3; 613/235-4402, 9940; Fax: 613/235-1176; Military Attachés Section: #1125, 90 Sparks St., Ottawa ON K1P 5B4; 613/230-7660; Ambassador, His Excellency

Fernando Urrutia; Counsellor, Luis Palma; **Edmonton**: Hon. Consul, Domingo Chavez, 7912-104 St. Edmonton AB T6E 4C8, 403/439-9838; Fax: 403/433-2376; **Montreal**: Consul General, Miguel Poklepovic: #710, 1010, rue Sherbrooke ouest, Montreal PQ H3A 2R7, 514/499-0405; **Toronto**: Consul General, Rene Faraggi, #800, 170 Bloor St. W. Toronto ON M5R 3L9, 416/924-0106; Fax: 416/924-9563; **Vancouver**: Consul, General, Dennis J. Biggs, #1250, 1185 Georgia St. W., Vancouver BC V6E 4E6, 604/681-9162; Fax: 604/682-2445; **Winnipeg**: Hon. Consul, Dr. Fernardo Guijon, 59 Emily St., Winnipeg MB R3E 1Y9, 204/787-4259; Fax: 204/889-4410

People's Republic of China
Embassy of China: 515 St. Patrick St. **Ottawa** ON K1N 5H3; 613/789-3434; Fax: 613/789-1911; Ambassador, His Excellency Zhang Yijun; Counsellor, Chen Wenzhou; Counsellor Commercial Affairs, Yu Zhiting; Counsellor Science and Technology, Huang Xing; Toronto: Consul General, Tang Fuquan, 240 Saint George St., **Toronto** ON M5R 2P4, 416/964-7260; Fax: 416/324-6468; **Vancouver**: Consul General, Yang Zongliang, 3380: Granville St. Vancouver BC V6H 3K3; 604/734-7492; Fax: 604/737-0154

Republic of Columbia
Embassy of Columbia: #1002, 360 Albert St., **Ottawa** ON K1R 7X7; 613/230-3760; Fax: 613/230-4416; Ambassador, His Excellency Alfonso Lopez Caballero; Minister-Counsellor, Hector Caceres; **Montreal**: Consul, Eufracio Morales: #420, 1010 rue Sherbrooke ouest, Montreal PQ H3A 2R7, 514/849-4852; Fax: 514/849-4324; **Toronto**: Consul General, Clara Maria Leon;

#2108, 1 Dundas St. W., Toronto ON M5G 1Z3; 416/977-0098; Fax: 416/977-1025; Toronto, Consul, Commercial Section, James Clemenger; #315, 4100 Yonge St., Toronto ON M2B 2B5, 416/512-9212; Fax: 416/512-9458; **Vancouver**: Hon. Consul, William Bush; 890 789 West Pender St., Vancouver BC V6C 1H2; 604/685-6435; Fax: 604/685-6485

Republic of the Congo

Embassy of the Congo (to Canada): 4891 Colorado Ave., NW. **Washington** DC 20011; 202/726-5500; Fax: 202/726-1860; Telex: 197370; Ambassador, His Excellency P.D. Boussoukou-Boumba; Counsellor, Economic Affairs, Ikourou Yoka; Pointe Clare: Hon. Consul, Marcel P. Rigny, 2 Cedar Ave., Pointe Clare PQ H9S 4Y1; 514/697-3781; Fax: 514/697-9860

Republic of Costa Rica

Embassy of Costa Rica: #208, 135 York St., **Ottawa** ON K1N 5T4; 613/562-2855; Fax: 613/562-2582; Ambassador, His Excellency Carlos Miranda; Minister-Counsellor, Francisco Gonzalez; Montreal: Consul General, Monserrat Romero-Royo, 1425, boul René Lévesque Ouest, **Montreal** PQ H3G 1T7; 514/393-1057; Fax: 514/393-1624; **Saskatoon**: Hon. Consul General, Ricardo Campbell, 245 Clearwater Ct., Saskatoon SK S7K 3Y9, 306/ 955-6000; Fax: 416/961-6771; **Toronto**: Hon. Consul, Peter-Alexander Kircher; 164 Avenue Road, Toronto ON M5R 2H9, 416/961-6773; Fax: 416/ 961-6771; **Vancouver**: Hon. Consul, General, William A. Dow, 804, 1550 Alberni St., Vancouver BC V6G 1A5, 604/669-0797; Fax: 604/669-4659

Republic of Croatia

Embassy of Croatia: #1700, 130 Albert St., **Ottawa** ON K1P 5G4; 613/230-7351; Fax: 613/230-7388; Ambassador, His Excellency Zeljko Urban; Minister-Counsellor. Ljerka Alajbeg; Counsellor, Economic, Vesela Mrdjen; First Secretary & Consul, Hrvoje Sagrak; **Mississauga**: Consul General, Ivan Picukaric; #302, 918 Dundas St., East Mississauga ON L4Y 2B8; 905/277-9051; Fax: 905/277-5432

Republic of Cuba

Embassy of Cuba: 388 Main St., **Ottawa** ON K1S 1E3; 613/563-0141; Fax: 613/563-0068; Email: cuba@iosphere.net; Ambassador, His Excellency Bievenido Garcia Negrin; Minister-Counsellor, Jorge Lamadrid Mascaro; Third Secretary, Deborah Ojeda Valedon; **Montreal**: Consul General, Gabriel Tiel, 1415 Pine Ave. West. Montreal PQ H3G 2B2, 514/843-8897; Fax: 845-1063; **Toronto**: Consul General, Jose Menendez, #401, 5353 Dundas St. W. Toronto ON. M9B 6H8; 416/234-8181; Fax: 416/234-2754

Republic of Cyprus

High Commission for Cyprus (to Canada): c/o Republic of Cyprus: 2211 R. St., NW, **Washington** DC 20008; 202/462-5772; Fax: 202/483-6710; High Commissioner, His Excellency Andreas J. Jacovides; Counsellor, Leonidas Markides; **Calgary**: Hon. Consul, Alfred A. Balm, 3900 Bankers Hall, 855-2 St. SW Calgary AB T2P 4J8; 403/264-3400; Fax: 403/237-8675; **Montreal**: Hon. Consul, Dr. Michael P. Paidoussis; #PH2, 2930, boul Edourard Montpetit, Montreal PQ H3T 1J7; 514/735-7233; Fax: 514/398-7365; **To-**

ronto: Consul General, Archilleas Antoniades, Cypress Consulate, #1010, Box 43, 365 Bloor St. East Toronto ON M4W 3L4; 413/944-0998; Fax: 416/944-9149; **Winnipeg**: Hon. Consul, Costas P. Ataliotis; 1430 Ellice Ave., Winnipeg MB R3G 0G4, 204/774-6724; Fax: 204/774-2002

Czech Republic

Embassy of the Czech Republic: 541 Sussex Dr., **Ottawa** ON K1N 6Z6; 613/562-3875; Fax: 613/562-3878; Ambassador, His Excellency Stanislav Chylek; Counsellor, Vaclav Prosec; First Secretary, Economic & Trade Affairs, Jaroslav Zeman; Culture & Press Affairs, Nora Jurkovicova; Consul, Eva Hendrychova; **Montreal**: Consul General, Petr Dokladal, 1305, av Pine Ouest, Montreal PQ H3G 1B2, 514/849-4495; Fax: 849-4117; **Vancouver**: Hon. Consul, Miroslav F.M. Hermann; #2100, 1111 West Georgia St., PO Box 48800, Vancouver BC V7X 1K9; 604/661-7530; Fax: 688-0829

Kingdom of Denmark

Embassy of Denmark: #450, 46 Clarence St., **Ottawa** ON K1N 9K1; 613/562-1811; Fax: 613/562-1812; Ambassador, His Excellency Jorgen M. Behnke; Minister-Counsellor, Otto H. Larsen; **Calgary**: Hon. Consul, Kai Mortensen, 1235-11 Ave. SW Calgary AB T3C 0M5; 403/245-5755; Fax: 403/228-6739; **Edmonton**: Hon. Consul, Donn Larsen; Oxford Tower, #1112, 10235-101 St., Edmonton AB T5J 1G1; 403/426-1457; Fax: 403/420-0005; **Halifax**: Hon. Consul of Denmark, H.I. Mathers, 1525 Birmingham St., P.O. Box 3550 South, Halifax NS B3J 3J3, 902/429-5221; Telex: 019-21771; **Montreal**: Hon. Consul, Michel Blouin, 1 Place Ville Marie, 35 Fl., Montreal

PQ H3B 4M4; 514/871-8977; Regina: Consul, Inge Ryan, MacPherson, Leslie & Tyerman, 1919 Saskatchewan Dr. 6th Fl., Regina SK S4P 3V7; 306/787-4750; Fax: 306/787-3989; **St. John's**: Hon. Consul, Peter Norman Outerbridge, 92 Elizabeth Ave, P.O. Box 6150, St. John's NF A1C 5X8; 709/726-0020; Fax: 709/726-6013; **Toronto**: Consul General, Poul Larsen, #310, 151 Bloor St. West, Toronto ON M5S 1S4; 416/962-5661; Fax: 604/684-8054; **Winnipeg**: Hon. Consul, Anders Bruun, 239 Aubert St., Winnipeg MB R2H 3J8; 204/233-8541; Fax: 204/942-0570

Republic Of Djibouti
c/o Embassy of the Republic of Djibouti: #515, 1156-15th St., NW, **Washington** DC 20005; 202/331-0270; Fax: 202/331-0302; Telex: 4490085 AMDJ US; Ambassador, His Excellency Roble Olhaye; Counsellor, Dysane Dorani

Commonwealth of Dominica c/o Organization of the Eastern Cari bbean States

Dominican Republic
Edmonton: Hon. Consul, Robert W. Hladun, #100, 10187-104 St., Edmonton AB, 403/423-1888; Fax: 403/424-0934; **Montreal**: Consul General, Esmerelda Villanueva; Central Tower 1055 St. Mattieu, bur. 241, Montreal PQ H3H 2S3, 514/933-9008; Fax: 514/933-2070; **Saint John**: Hon. Consul, John Driscoll, 59 Broad St., Saint John NB E2L 1Y3; **St. John's**: Hon Consul, M.G. Renouf, 10 Forest Ave., St. John's NF A1C 3J9; **Vancouver**: Hon. Vice-

Consul, Andrew H.S. Leung, #616, 1155 West Georgia St., Vancouver BC V6E 3H4, 604/683-8033

Organization of the Eastern Caribbean States
High Commission for the Countries of the Eastern Caribbean States: #1610, 112 Kent St., **Ottawa**, ON. K1P 5P2. 613/236-8952; Fax: 613/236-3042. Acting High Commissioner. Jean-Francois Michel. First Secretary, Political & Consular. C.O. Dasent. Includes: Antigua & Barbuda, Commonwealth of Dominica, Grenada, Montserrat, Saint Christopher (Saint Kitts) & Nevis, Saint Lucia, Saint Vincent & the Grenadines.

Republic of Ecuador
Embassy of Ecuador: #1311. 50 O'Conner St., **Ottawa**, ON. K1P 6L2. 613/563-8206; Fax: 613/235-5776; Email: MECUACAN@INASEC.CA. Ambassador. His Excellency Alfredo Crespo Cordero. Counsellor, Rafeal Paredes. **Montreal**: Consul General, Gabriel Garcés, #440, 1010 rue Ste Catherine ouest, Montreal, PQ. H3B 3R3. 514/874-4071; Fax: 514/874-4071. Okotoks: Hon. Consul. Gordon Lentz, AB Consulate, PO Box 29, Site 6, RR#1, Okotoks AB. T0L 1T0. 403/938-8142. Richmond: Hon. Consul. Etienne Walter. #802, 7100 Gilbert Rd., Richmond, BC. V7C 5C3. 604/273-8577; Fax: 604/273-8576. **Toronto**: Consul General, Francisco Martinez. #470, 151 Bloor St. West, Toronto, ON. M5S 1S4. 416/968-2077; Fax: 416/968-3348.

Arab Republic of Egypt

Embassy of Egypt: 454 Laurier Ave. East, **Ottawa**, ON. K1N 6R3. 613/
234-4931; Fax: 613/234-9347 Commercial Office: #207, 85 Range Rd.,
Ottawa, ON. K1N 8J6. 613/238-6263; Fax: 613/238-2578. Ambassador,
His Excellency Mahmoud Farghal. Minister Plenipotentiary, Teymour
Moustapha Sirry. Counsellor, Ibrahim Khairat. **Montreal**: Consul General,
Dr Mohamed Ismail. #2617, 1, Place Ville Marie, Montreal PQ. H3B 4S3.
514/866-8455; Fax: 514/866-0835.

Republic of El Salvador

Embassy of El Salvador: #504, 209 Kent St. **Ottawa** ON K2P 1Z8; 613/238-
2939; Fax: 613/238-6940; Ambassador, Alfredo F. Ungo; Minister-
Counsellor, Celine Quinteros; Montreal: Consul-General, Mauricio Suarez-
Escalante, 4330 Sherbrooke ouest, Montreal PQ H3Z 1E1; 514/934-3678;
Fax: 934-3706; **Toronto**: Consul, Joaquin Antonio Zaldivar, #320, 151 Bloor
St. West Toronto ON M5S 1T6, 416/975-0812; Fax: 416/975-0283;
Vancouver: Hon. Consul, Jeffery Rodd Moore, Sinclair Center, P.O. Box 649,
Stn. A. Vancouver BC V6C 2N5; 604/732-8142

Eritrea

Embassy of Eritrea (to Canada): #400, 910-17th St. NW, **Washington** DC
20006; 202/429-1991; Fax: 202/429-90004; Ambassador, Vacant. **Ottawa**:
Second Secretary and Consul. Nura Mohammed Omer. #610, 75 Albert St.,
Ottawa ON. K1P 5E7. 613/234-3989; Fax: 613/234-6213

Republic of Estonia

Embassy of Estonia (to Canada): #1000, 1030 - 16th St. NW. **Washington** DC 20005. 202/789-0320; Fax: 202/789-0471. Ambassador: His Excellency Toomas H. Iives. **Toronto**: Hon. Consul. General, Ilmar Heinsoo. #202, 958 Broadview Ave., Toronto, ON. M4K 2R6. 416/461-0764; Fax: 416/461-0448

Democratic Republic of Ethiopia

Embassy of Federal Democratic Republic of Ethiopia: #210, 151 Slater St., **Ottawa**, ON. K1P 5H3. 613/235-6637; Fax: 613/2235-4638. Email: infoethi@magi.com Ambassador, His Excellency Dr. Fedacu Gadamu. Counsellor, Wahide Baley. Third Secretary, Beleyou Kifelew

European Union

Delegation of the European Commission in Canada: #330, 111 Albert St., **Ottawa**, ON. K1P 1A5. 613/238-6464; Fax: 613/238-5191. Ambassador & Head of Delegation, His Excellency Jean-Pierre Juneau

Commission of the European Communities

Delegation of the Commission of the European Communities: #1110, 350 Sparks St., **Ottawa** ON K1R 7S8; 613/238-6464; Fax: 613/238-5191; Ambassador & Head of Delegation, His Excellency John R. Beck; Attaché, David Tyson; Counsellor, Economic and Commercial Affairs, Carlos Freitas da Silva

Fiji

Embassy of Fiji (to Canada): One United Nations Plaza, 26th Fl., **New York**, NY 10017; 212/355-7316; Fax: 212/319-1896; Ambassador, His Excellency Manasa K. Seniloli; **Ottawa**: Hon. Consul. Dr. D. Elaine Pressman, #750, 130 Slater St., Ottawa ON; 613/233-9252; **Vancouver**: Hon. Consul. Raj Gopal Pillai, 1840 Clark Dr., Vancouver BC V5N 3G4, 604/254-5544

Republic of Finland

Embassy of Finland: #850, 55 Metcalfe St., **Ottawa** ON K1P 6L5; 613/236-2389; Fax: 613/-238-1474; Ambassador, His Excellency Veijo Sampovaara; First Secretary (Deputy Head of Mission), Roy Eriksson; **Calgary**: Hon. Consul, Judith M. Romanchuk, Home Oil Tower, #702, 324-8 Ave. SW, Calgary AB T2P- 2Z2, 403/426-7865; Fax: 403/428-6964; **Halifax**: Hon. Consul. Frank metcalf, Benjamin Wier House, 1459 Hollis St., Halifx NS B3J 1V1,902/420-1990; Fax: 902/429-1171; **Montréal**: Hon. Consul. James G. Wright, Stock Exchange Tower, #3400, 800 Place Victoria, PO Box 242, Montréal PQ H4Z 139, 514/397-7437; Fax: 514/397-7600; **Québec**: Hon. Consul. Henri Grondin, Edifice Mérci, #200, 801, ch St-Louis, Québec PQ G1S 1C1, 418/683-3000; Fax: 418/683-8784; **Regina**: Hon. Consul. Gordon J. Kuski, Royal Bank Bldg., #700, 2010 - 11th Ave., Regina SK S4P 0J3, 306/757-1641; Fax: 306/359-0785; **Saint John**: Hon. Consul. Thomas L. McGloan, PO Box 7174, Stn A. Saint John NB E2L 4S6, 506/634-7450; Fax: 506/634-3612; **Sault Ste. Marie**: Hon. Consul. Raimo Vitala, 29 Pageant Dr., Sault St. Marie ON P6B 5J7, 705/924-6196; **Sudbury**: Hon. Consul. R. Hannu Piironen, 176 McNaughton St., Sudbury ON B3E 1V3, 705/675-0067;

Fax: 705/675-0067;**Thunder Bay**: Hon. Consul. Seppo K. Paivalainen, Gordon, Vauthier, Paivalainen, 275 Bay St., Thunder Bay ON P7B 1R7, 807/343-9394; Fax: 807/344-1562; **Timmins**: Hon. Consul. Margaret Kangas, 5 Birch St. North, Timmins ON P4N 68C, 705/264-7857; Fax: 705/264-9977; **Toronto**: Consul. Helena Lappalainen, #604, 1200 Bay St., Toronto, ON M5R 2A5, 416/964-0066; Fax: 416/964-1524; Telex: 062-2513; **Vancouver**: Hon. Consul General Lars-Henrik Wrede, #1100, 1188 Georgia St. West, Vancouver BC V6E 4A2, 604/687-8237; Telex: 04-55703; **Winnipeg**: Hon. Consul. Robert Purves, #127, 167 Lombard Av., Winnipeg MB R3B 0T6, 204/942-7457; Fax: 204/942-7458

France

Embassy of France: 42 Sussex Dr., Ottawa ON K1M 2C9 613/789-1795; Fax: 613/789-3484; Ambassador, His Excellency Alfred Siefer-Gaillardin; Minister-Counsellor, Jean François Vallette; Counsellor, Cultura Affairs, Michel Deverge; Counsellor, Economic & Commercial Affairs, Alain Nourissier; Chicoutimi: Hon. Consul. François Brochet, 1596, Bégin, Chicoutimi PQ G7H 5T6, 418/549-2195; **Edmonton**: Consul General, Pierre Marchal, Highfield Place, #300, 10010-106 St., Edmonton AB T5J 3L8, 403/428-0232, 0235; Fax: 403/426-1450; **Halifax**: Hon. Consul, Roland Bonnel, 6234 Lawrence St., Halifax NS B3L 1J9, 902/494-2319; **Moncton**: Consul General, Gérard Perrolet, 250 Lutz St., PO Box 1109, Moncton NB E1C 8P6, 506/857-4191; Fax: 506/858-8169; Montréal: Consul General, Gérard Leroux, #2601, 1, Place Ville Marie, Montréal PQ H3B 4S3, 514/878-4381; Fax: 514/878-3981; Telex: 052-44890; Commercial Section: #2710, 1000, rue de la

Gauchetière ouest, 27e étage, Montréal, PQ, H3B 4W5, 514/878-9851; Fax: 514/878-3677; Telex: 055-61219; **North Sydney**: Hon. Vice Consul, Thérèse Goora, North Sydney Consulate, 190 Brook St., PO Box 308, North Sydney NS B2A 3M4, 902/794-3676; Québec: Consul General, Dominique de Combles de Nayves, Kent House, 25, rue St-Louis, Québec PQ G1R 3Y8, 418/694-2294; Fax: 418/694-2297; Cultural & Scientific Affairs: 25, rue St-Louis, Québec PQ G1R 3Y8, 418/688-0430; **Saskatoon**: Hon. Consul, Bernard M. Michel, Saskatoon Consulate, Cameco Corporation, 2121 - 11th St. West, Saskatoon SK S7M 1J3, 306/956-6305; Fax: 306/956-6302; **St. John's**: Hon. Vice Consul, Pierre Morin, St. John's Consulate, 19 Diefenbaker St., St. John's NF A1A 2M2, 709/737-8924; **Sudbury**: Hon. Consul, Onésime Tremblay, Sudbury Consulate, 1101 Ramsey lake Rd., Site 3, PO Box 18, Sudbury ON P3E 5J2, 705/674-8503; **Toronto**: Vice Consul, Cultural Affairs & Co-operation, Frédéric Limare, #400, 130 Bloor St. West, Toronto, ON M5H 3R3, 416/925-8041; Fax: 416/925-3076; Visa Section: 416/925-8233; Commercial Section: #2004, 20 Queen St. West, Toronto, ON, M5H 3R3, 416/977-1257; Fax: 416/977-7944; **Vancouver**: Consul General and Cultural Affairs, Maryse Beriau, The Vancouver Bldg., #1201, 736 Granville St., Vancouver BC V6Z 1H9, 604/681-4345; Fax: 604/681-4287; Commercial Section: 604/681-5875; Fax: 604/681-4287; **Victoria**: Hon. Consul, Gordon Denford, 1162 Fort St., Victoria BC V8V 3K8, 250/385-1505; Fax: 250/385-9851; **Whitehorse**: Hon. Consul. Rolf Hougen, 305 Main St., Whitehorse YT Y1A 2B4, 403/667-4222; Fax: 403/668-6328; Telex: 036-8274; **Winnipeg**: Hon. Consul. Frédéric Granger, Winnipeg Consulat, 64 Athlone Dr., Winnipeg MB R3J 3L2, 204/837-9583

Gabonese Republic

Embassy of Gabon: 4 Range Rd., **Ottawa** ON K1N 8J3, 613/232-5301/02; Fax: 613/232-6916; Telex: 053-4295; AMBGAB OTT; Ambassador, His Excellency Alphonse Oyabi-Gnala; Counsellor, Economic & Financial Affairs, Lucien Moubouvi; **Montréal**: Hon. Consul, Luc Benoit, 85, rue Ste-Catherine ouest, Montréal PQ H2X 3P4, 514/287-8500; Fax: 514/287-8643; Telex: 055-60122;

Republic of the Gambia

High Commission for Gambia (to Canada): c/o Gambia Embassy; #1000, 1155 - 15th St., NW, **Washington** DC 20005; 202/785-1399. Fax: 202/785-1430; Email: saidy@gambia.com; High Commissioner, Vacant; Chargé d'affaires, His Excellency Tombong Saidy; Montréal PQ H3P 1K8, 514/731-5775; Fax: 514/731-4374; **Vancouver**: Hon. Consul of Gambia, U. Gary Charlwood, #900, 1199 West Pender St., Vancouver BC V6E 2R1, 604/662-3800; Fax: 604/662-3878

Federal Republic of Germany

Embassy of Germany: 1 Waverley St. **Ottawa** ON K2P 0T8; 614/232-1101; Fax: 613/594-9330; Email: bn555@frenet.carleton.ca; 1000440.64@compuserve.com; Postal Address: PO Box 369, Stn A, Ottawa ON K1N 8V4; Ambassador, His Excellency Dr. Hans-Guenter Sulimma; Minister-Counsellor, Dr. Juergen Hellner; Counsellor, Cultural Affairs, Charlotte Schwarzer; Counsellor, Economic & Commercial Affairs, Ulrich Grau; Counsellor, Press& Information Office, Ulrich Koehn; Defence Attaché, Lt.

Col. Christian Ibrom; **Calagary**: Hon. Consul, Osmar Bletzner, #1970, 700 - 4th Ave. SW, Calgary AB T2P 3J4, 404/260-5900; Fax: 403/269-5901; **Fort St. John**: Hon. Consul, Friedrich Eduard Hermann von Ilberg, #9832, 98 A Avenue, Fort St. John BCV1J 1S2, 250/785-4300; Fax: 250/785-5028; **Halifax**: Hon. Consul, Prof. Edgar Gold, Bank of Commerce Bldg., #708, 1809 Barrington St., Halifax NX B3J 3K8, 902/420-1599; Fax: 902/422-4713; Telex: 019-21593; **Kitchener**: Hon. Consul, Peter D. Krise. 385 Frederick St., Kitchener ON N2H 2P2, 519/745-6149; Fax: 519/576-0591; **London**: Hon. Consul, Barbara Weis, 71 Wharncliff Rd. South, London ON N5J 2J8, 519/432-4133; Fax: 519/667-5187; **Montréal**: Consul General, Friz von Rottenburg, 1250, boul René-Lévesque ouest, Montréal PQ H3B 4W8, 514/931-2277; Fax: 514/931-7239; **Regina**: Hon. Consul, Guenter Kocks, 3534 Argyle Rd., Regina SK S4S 2B8, 306/586-8762; Fax: 306/586-8762; St. John's: Hon. Consul, Gunter K. Sann, 22 Poplar Ave., St. John's NF A1B 1C8, 709/753-7777; Fax: 709/739-6666; **Toronto**: Consul General, Roland Fournes, 77 Admiral Rd., Toronto ON M5R 2L4, 416/925-2813; Fax: 416/925-2818; Telex: 06-22866; **Vancouver**: Consul General, Franz-Josef Meurer, World Trade Centre, #704, 999 Canada Place, Vancouver BC V6C 3E1,604/684-8377, 684-4258 (Visas); Fax: 604/684-8334; Telex: 04-507769; **Winnipeg**: Hon. Consul, Gerhard Spindler, #208, 310 Donald St., Winnipeg MB R3B 2H4, 204/947-0958; Fax: 204/669-6197

Republic of Ghana
High Commission for Ghana: 1 Clemow Ave., **Ottawa** ON K1S 2A9; 613/236-0871/3; Fax: 613/236-0874; High Commissioner, His Excellency Annan

Arkyin Cato; Counsellor, C.K. de Souza; **Montréal**: Hon. Consul-General, Joachim Normand, #900, 1420 Sherbrooke St. West, Montréal PQ H3G 1K3, 514/849-1417; Fax: 514/849-2643; **North Vancouver**: Hon. Consul-General, Dr. William Herbert Lawrence Allsopp, 2919 Eddystone Cr., North Vancouver BC V7H 1B8, 604/929-1496; Fax: 604/929-1860

Grenada *c/o* Organization of the Eastern Caribbean States
Toronto: Consul General, Adrian C.A. Hayes, #820, 439 University Ave., Toronto ON M5G 1Y8, 416/595-1343; Fax: 416/595-8278; **Winnipeg**: Hon. Consul, Caspar A. Shade, 10 Rice Rd., Winnipeg MB R3T 3N4, 204/269-4788; Fax: 204/452-8491

Republic of Guatemala
Embassy of Guatemala: #1010, 130 Albert St., **Ottawa** ON K1P 5G4; 613/233-7188; Fax: 613/233-0135; Consular Section: 613/233-7188; Ambassador, His Excellency Francisco Villagran de Leon; Minister-Counsellor, Carmen Aida Aguilera; **Norval**: Hon. Consul, Roberto Sierra, PO Box 319, Norval ON L0P 1K0, 416/604-0655; **Vancouver**: Consul General, Vacant, #760, 777 Hornby St., Vancouver BC V6Z 1S4, 604/688-5209; Fax: 688-5210

Republic of Guinea
Embassy of Guinea: 483 Wilbrod St., **Ottawa** ON K1N 6N1; 61/789-8444; Fax: 513/789-7560; Ambassador, His Excellency Thierno Habib Diallo; First Secretary, Jeanne Bangoura; **Calgary**: Hon. Consul, Giovanni De Maria, AB Consulate, 79 Willamette Dr. SE, Calgary AB T2J 2A3, 403/225-2956; Fax:

403/225-2957; **Toronto**: Hon. Consul, Charles Arthur Downes, 1 St. John's Rd., Toronto ON M6P 4C7, 416/656-4812; Fax: 416/767-6070; **Vancouver**: Hon. Consul, Raymond L. Saunders, 123 Cambie St., Vancouver BC V6B 4R3, 604/327-5550; Fax: 604/684-2100

Republic of Guinea-Bissau
Embassy of Guinea-Bissau (to Canada): 918 - 16th St. NW, Mezzanine Suite, **Washington** DC 20006; 202/872-4222; Ambassador, His Excellency Alfredo Lopes Cabral; **Montréal**: Hon. Consul, Nicolas M. Matte, Place Mercantile, 770, rue Sherbrooke ouest, Montréal PQ H3A 1G1, 514/842-9831; Fax: 514/288-7389

Co-operative Republic of Guyana
Burnside Building: #309, 151 Slater St., **Ottawa** ON K1P 5H3; 613/235-7249; Fax: 613/235-1447; HighCommissioner, His Excellency Brindley H. Benn; First Secretary, Jennifer Wills; **Willowdale**: Hon. Consul, Geoffrey Da Silva, #206, 505 Consumers Rd., Willowdale ON M2J 4V8, 416/404-6040; Fax: 416/494-1530

Republic of Haiti
Embassay of Haiti: Tour B, Place de Ville; #205, 112 Kent St., Ottawa ON K1P 5P2; 613/238-1628; Fax: 613/238-2986; Ambassador, His Excellency Emmanuel Ambroise; Minister/Counsellor, Lhande J. Henriquez; Montréal: Consul, Luciano Pharaon, #1335, 1801 av McGill College, 13e étage, Montréal PQ H3A 2N4, 514/499-1919; Fax: 514/499-1818

Republic of Honduras

Embassy of Honduras: #908, 151 Slater St., **Ottawa** ON K1P 5H3; 613/233-8900; Fax: 613/232-0193; Email: scastell@magmacom.com; breina@magmacom.com; Ambassador, His Excellency Salomé Casstellanos Delgado; Counsellor, Commercial, Bertha M. Reina; First Secretary & Consular Affairs, Marco Tulio Romero; Attaché, Press, Patricia Osorio; **Montréal**: Chancellor, Manuel Urbina Bulnes, #306, 1650, boul de Maisonneuve Ouest, Montréal PQ H3H 2P3, 514/937-1138; **Québec**: Hon. Consul, Thérèse Lacroix, 1334 Maréchal Foch, Québec PQ G1S 2C4, 418/681-5070; **Vancouver**: Hon. Consul, Enrique Gonzalez-Calvo, #1026, 510 West Hasting St., Vancouver BC V6B 1L8, 614/685-7711

Hellenic Republic

Embassy of Greece: 76-80 MacLaren St., Ottawa ON K2P 0K6; 613/238-6271; Fax: 613/238-5676; Ambassador, His Excellency John Thomoglou; Counsellor, Constantine Giovas; **Montréal**: Consul General, Nicholas Vamvounakis, 1170, Place du Frère André, 3e étage, Montréal PQ H3B 3C6, 514/875-2119; Fax: 514/875-8781; Telex: 044-60963 GREEK CONS MTL; **Toronto**: Consul General, Christos Kontovounissios, #1300, 365 Bloor St. East, Toronto ON M4W 3L4, 416/515-0133; Fax: 416/515-0209; **Vancouver**: Consul, Helen Sourani, 3501, 1200 Burrard St., Vancouver BC V6Z 2C7, 604/681-1381; Fax: 604/681-6656

Republic of Hungary

Embassy of Hungary: 299 Waverley St., OttawaON K2P 0V9; 613/230-

2717; Fax: 613/230-7560; Email: ATTMAILHUEMBOTT; Ambassador, His Excellency Károly Gedai; Minister Plenipotentiary, István Torzsa; Head, Consular Section, Norbert Konkoly; **Calgary**: Hon. Consul, Béla Balázs, 1700 - 96 Ave. SW, Calgary AB T2V 5E5, 403/259-0052; Fax: 403/262-8343; **Montréal**: Consul. Judit Nolipa, #2040, 1200, av McGill Collège, Montréal PQ H3B 4G7, 514/393-1048; Fax: 514/393-8226; **Toronto**: Consul General, Lajos Illich, #1115, 121 Bloor St. East, Toronto ON M4W 3M5, 416/923-8981; Fax: 416/923-2732; **Vancouver**: Hon. Consul, André Molnár, 165-West 2nd Ave., Vancouver BCV6J 4R2, 604/734-6698; Vancouver: Hon. Vic-Consul, Brigitte A. Farkas, #203, 1076 Richards St., Vancouver BC V6B 3E1, 604/691-5936; Fax: 604/691-3466

Republic of Iceland
Embassy of Iceland (to Canada): #1200, 1156 - 15 St. NW, **Washington** DC 20005; 202/265-6653; Fax: 202/265-6656; Email: idemb.wash@utn.stjr.is; Ambassador, His Excellency Einar Benediktsson; Minister-Counsellor, Petur G. Thorsteinsson; **Edmonton**: Hon. Consul, Gudmundur A. Arnason, 14434 McQueen Rd., Edmonton AB T5N 3L6, 403/455-7946; **Montréal**: Hon. Consul General, William I.M. Turner Jr., #575/ 1981, av McGill Collège, Montréal PQ H3A 2X1, 514/982-0188; Fax: 514/982-0190; **Ottawa**: Hon. Consul General, E.T. Lahey, #300, 246 Queen St., Ottawa ON L1P 5E4, 613/238-7412; Fax: 613/238-1799; **Regina**: Hon. Consul, Jon Orn Jonsson, 4705 Castle Rd., Regina SK S4S 4W9, 306/586-7737; Fax: 306/359-1885; **St. John's**: Hon. Consul, Avalon M. Goodridge, 20 Glasgow Place, St. John's NF A1B 2B4, 709/753-2787; Fax: 709/754-0699; **Timberlea**: Hon. Consul,

Lawrence J. Cooke, 14 Bay Ct., Timberlea NS B3T 1C4, 902/876-0657; Fax: 902/876-0657; **Toronto**: Hon. Consul, J. Ragnar Johnson, #2400, 250 Yonge St., Toronto ON M5B 2M6, 416/979-6740; Fax: 416-979-1234; **West Vancouver**: Hon. Consul, Heather Alda Ireland, 940 Younette Dr., West Vancouver BC V7T 1S9 , 604/922-0854; Fax: 604/925-2524; **Winnipeg**: Hon. Consul General, Neil Bardal, 984 Portage Ave., Winnipeg MB R3G 0R6, 204/949-2200; Fax: 204/783-5916

Republic of India
High Commission of India: 10 Springfield Rd., **Ottawa** ON K1M 1C9, 613/744-3751; Fax: 613/744-0913; Email: hicomind@Ottawa.net; High Commissioner, His Excellency Prem Kumar Budhwar; High Commissioner (Designate), His Excellency G.S. Bedi; Deputy High Commissioner & Minister, AlK. Banerjee; **Toronto**: Consul General, Rajiv Kumar Bhatia, #500, 2 Bloor St. West, Toronto ON M4W 3E2, 416/960-0751, 2377; Fax: 416/960-9812; Email: cgindia@pathcom.com; **Vancouver**: Consul General, Jawahar Lal, 325 Howe St., 2nd Fl., Vancouver BC V6C 1Z7, 614/662-8811; Fax: 604/682-2471; Email: indiaadm@axionet.com

Republic of Indonesia
55 Parkdale Ave., **Ottawa** ON K1Y 1E5, 613/724-1100; Fax: 613/724-1105; Email: kbri@prica.org; Ambassador, His Excellency Benjamin Parwoto; Counsellor, Economic, Chaidir Siregar; **Toronto**: Consul, Titiek S.A. Suyono, 129 Jarvis St., Toronto ON M5C 2H6, 416/360-4020; Fax: 416/360-4295;

Vancouver: Consul, Jacky D. Wahyu, 1455 West Georgia St., 2nd Fl. Vancouver BC V6G 2T3, 604/682-8855; Fax: 604/662-8396

Islamic Republic of Iran
Embassy of the Islamic Republic of Iran: 245 Metcalfe St., **Ottawa** ON K2P 2K2, 613/235-4726; Fax: 613/232-5712; Email: iranemb@sonetis.com; Deputy Chief of Mission, Parvis Afshari; Ambassador, HisExcellency M.H. Lavassani

Republic of Iraq
Embassy of Iraq: 215 McLeod St., **Ottawa** ON K2P 0Z8, 613/236-9177; Fax: 613/567-1101; Ambassador, Vacant; Chargé d'Affaires, Haitham Taufiq Al-Najjar; Attaché, Mohammed Fakhri

Ireland
Embassy of Ireland: #1105, 130 Albert St., **Ottawa** ON K1P 5G4, 613/233-6281; Fax: 613/233-5835; Ambassador, His Excellency Paul Dempsey; First Secretary, Ronan Corvin; Third Secretry, Stephen Dawson

State of Israel
Embassy of Israel: #1005, 50 O'Connor St., **Ottawa** ON L1P 6L2, 613/657-6450; Fax: 613/237-8865; Chargé d'Affaires, Eli Yerushalmi; **Montréal**: Consul General, Daniel Gal, #2620, 1155, boul René-Lévesque ouest, Montréal PQ H3B 4S5, 514/393-9372; Fax: 514/393-8795; **Toronto**: Consul

General, Yehudi Kinar, #700, 180 Bloor St. West, Toronto ON M5S 2V6, 416/961-1126; Fax: 416/961-7737

Italian Republic
Embassy of Italy: 275 Slater St., 21st Fl., **Ottawa** ON K1P 5H9, 613/232-2401; Fax: 613/233-1484; Ambassador, His Excellency Andrea Negrotto; Minister-Counsellor, Sandro de Bernadin; **Brantford**: Hon. Vice Consul, Arangelo mrtino, 288 Murray St., Brantford ON N3S 5T1, 519/753-0404; **Calgary**: Hon. Consular Agent, Augusto Ambrosino, 326 - 27 Ave. NE, Calgary AB T2E 2A2, 403/248-3457; **Edmonton**: Vice Consul, Pierfrancesco De Cerchio, #1900, Midland Walwyn Tower, Edmonton Centre, Edmonton AB T5J 2Z2, 403/423-5153; Fax: 403/423-5214; **Guelph**: Hon. Vice-Consul, Imelda Porcellato, 127 Ferguson St., Guelph ON N1E 2Y9, 519/763-2228; **Halifax**: Hon. Vice Consul. Rodolfo Meloni, #7 1574 Argyle St., PO Box 12, Halifax NS B2J 2B3, 902/422-0066; **Hamilton**: Vice Consul, Salvatore Di Venezia, #509, 105 Main St., East, Hamilton ON L8N 1G6, 905/529-5030; Fax: 905/529-7028; **Kingston**: Hon. Vice Consul, Nicola A. d'Anna Sivilotti, 221 King St. East, Kingston ON K7L 3A6, 613/548-4380; **London**: Hon. Vice Consul Luigi Rossetti, 344 Richmond St. 2nd Fl., London, ON N6A 3C3, 519/438-6740; **Montréal**: Consul General, Carlo Selvaggi, 3489, av Drummond ouest, 2e étage, Montréal PQ H3G 1X6, 514/849-8351; Fax: 514/499-9471; **Niagara Falls**: Hon. Vice Consul, Domenico Morabito, 4904 Victoria Ave., Niagara Falls ON L2E 4C6, 905/356-2231; **Prince Rupert**: Hon. Consular Agent, Mario Giovanni Marogna, PO Box 640, Prince Rupert BC V8T 3S1, 250/624-6282; Fax: 250/624-6613; **Québec**: Hon. Consul, Riccardo Rossini,

355 - 23e rue, Québec PQ G1L 1W8,418/529-9801; Fax: 306/585-4894; **Regina**: Hon. Vice Consul, Lucia Papini, 82 Lowry Place, Regina SK S4S 4P5, 306/586-6832; Fax: 306/585-4894; **Sarnia**: Hon. Vice Consul, Antonio Domenichini, #210, 785 Exmouth St., Sarnia ON N1T 5P7, 519/336-0101; **Sault Ste. Marie**: Hon. Vice Consul, Rudolpho C. Peres, Professional Place, #201, 212 Queen St. East, Sault Ste. Marie ON P6A 5X8,705/949-0704; **St. John's**: Hon. Consular Agent, Gordon S. Lono, 8 Hunt Place, St. John's NF A1B 2J9, 709/730-8809; **Sudbury**: Hon. Vice Consul, Dr. Roberto Grosso, 96 Larch St., Sudbury ON P3E 1C1, 705/674-7922; **Sydney**: Hon. Consular Agent, Leonardo D'Addario, Sydney NS; **Thunder Bay**: Hon. Vice Consul, Giovanna Pirotta Zovatto, @205, 105 May St. North, Thunder Ban ON P7C 3N9, 807/622-9052; **Timmins**: Hon. Vice Consul, Rino Charles Bragagnolo, #131, 101 Mall, 38 Pine St. South, Timmins ON P4N 6K6, 705/264-1285; **Toronto**: Consul General, Leonardo Sampoli, 136 Beverley St., Toronto ON M5T 1Y5, 416/977-1566; Fax: 416/977-1119; **Trail**: Hon. Consular Agent, Gemma Merlo, 128 Colley st., Trail BC V1R 2M2, 250/364-1826; **Vancouver**: Consul General, Arnaldo Abeti, #705, 1200 Burrard St., Vancouver BC V6Z 2C7, 604/684-7288; Fax: 604/685-4263; **Victoria**: Hon. Vice Consul, Yolanda Pagnotta McKimmie, #207, 1050 Park Blvd., Victoria BC V8V 1T4, 250/386-3277; Fax: 2509/595-5812; **Windsor**: Hon. Vice Consul, Liliana Scotti Busi, 1145 Erie St. East, Windsor ON N9A 3Z6, 519/256-0092; **Winnipeg**: Hon. Vice Consul, Bruno Esposito, #309, 283 Protage Ave., Winnipeg MB R3B 2B5, 204/943-7637

Republic of Ivory Coast

Embassy of Ivory Coast: 9 Marlborough Ave., Ottawa ON K1N 8E6, 613/236-9919; Fax: 613/563-8287; Ambassador, His Excellency Julien Kacou; **Montréal**: Hon. Consul, André Vannerum, #602, 417, rue St-Pierre, Montréal PQ H2Y 2N4, 514/845-8121; Fax: 514/688-7473; **Toronto**: Hon. Consul, Peter J. Dawes, 260 Adelaide St. East, PO Box 110, Toronto ON M5A 1N1, 416/366-8490; Fax: 416/947-1534; **Vancouver**: Hon. Consul, Jim O'Hara, 1531 Haywood Ave. West, Vancouver BC V7W 1W4, 604/291-5182; Fax: 604/291-5225

Jamaica

Jamaican High Commission: #800, 275 Slater St., **Ottawa** ON K1P 5H9, 613/233-9311; Fax: 613/233-0611; High Commissioner, Her Excellency Maxine Eleanor Roberts; Counsellor, Ann Scott; First-Secretary, Caroline Blake; St. Albert: Hon. Consul Dolli Booth, 36 Windermere Cres., St. Albert AB T8N 3S5, 403/459-8440; **Toronto**: Consul General, Margarietta St. Juste, #482, 214 King St. West, Toronto ON M5H 3S6, 416/598-3008; **Winnipeg**: Hon. Consul, Prof. D.K. Gordon, 11 Wadham Bay, Winnipeg MB R3T 3K2, 204/269-5319

Japan

Embassy of Japan: 255 Sussex Dr., **Ottawa** ON K1N 9E6; 613/241-8541; Fax: 613/241-2232; Email: http://emb@japan.magi.com; Ambassador, His Excellency Takashi Tajima; Minister, Naoto Amaki; Minister, Kiyoshi Araki; Counsellor, Hiroshi Matsumura; **Edmonton**: Consul General, Shigeru Ise,

ManuLife Place, #2480, 10180 - 101 St., Edmonton AB T5J 3S4, 403/422-3752; Fax: 403/424-1635; **Halifax**: Hon. Consul General, Bruce S.C. Oland, Lindwood Holdings Ltd., Keith Hall, 1475 Hollis St., PO Box 2066, Halifax NS B3J 2Z1, 902/429-6530; **Montréal**: Consul General, Yuji Kurokawa, #2120, 600, rue de la Gauchetière ouest, Montrèal PQ H3B 4L8,514/866-3429; Fax: 514/395-6000; **Regina**: Hon. Consul General, Arthur Tsuneo Wakabayashi, 3234 Mountbatten Cres., Regina SK S4V 0Z4, 306/789-3221; Fax: 306/761-0766; **St. John's**: Hon. Consul General, Aidan Maloney, 2 Laughlin Cres., St. John's NF A1A 2G2, 709/722-3016; **Toronto**: Consul General, Hajime Tsujimoto, #2702, Toronto Dominion Bank Tower, Toronto Dominion Centre, PO Box 10, Toronto ON M5K 1A1, 416/363-7038; Fax: 416/367-9392; **Vancouver**: Consul General, Yasuo Nozaka, #900, 1177 Hastings St. West, Vancouver BC V6E 2K9, 604/684-5868; Fax: 604/684-6039; **Winnipeg**: Hon. Consul General, Otto Lang, 680 Wellington Cres., Winnipeg MB R3M 0C2, 204/284-0478

Hashemite Kingdom of Jordan
Embassy of Jordan: #701, 100 Bronson Ave., Ottawa ON K1R 6G8, 613/238-8090; Fax: 613/232-3341; Ambassador, Michael Molloy; Second Secretary, Karim Wael Masri

Republic of Kazakhstan
Consulate General of Kazakhstan: 7777 Keele St., **Concord** ON L4K 1Y7; Hon. Consul General, Robert P. Kaplan, P.C., Q.C., LL.B.

Republic of Kenya

High Commission for Kenya: 415 Laurier Ave. East, **Ottawa** ON K1N 6R4, 613/653-1773; Fax: 613/ 233-6599; High Commissioner, His Excellency Mwanyengela Ngali; Counsellor, Danielo Mayaka

Republic of Korea

Embassy of Korea: 151 Slater St., 5th Fl., **Ottawa** ON K1P 5H3, 613/232-1715; Fax: 613/232-0928; Ambassador, His Excellency Kee Bock Shin; Minister, Young-Jo Jung; **Montréal**: Consul General, Tae Kyu Yang, #2500, 1002, rue Sherbrooke ouest, Montréal PQ H3A 3G4,514/845-3243; Fax: 514/ 845-8517; **Toronto**: Consul General, Kyoung-Bo Shim, 555 Avenue Rd., Toronto ON M4V 2J7, 416/920-3809; Fax: 416/924-7305; **Vancouver**: Consul General, Johng Won Kang, #830, 1066 Hastings St. West, Vancouver BCV6E 3X1, 604/681-9581; Fax: 614/681-4864

State of Kuwait

Embassy of Kuwait: 80 Elgin St., **Ottawa** ON K1P 1C6, 513/780-9999; Fax: 613/780-9905; Ambassador, His Excellency Abdulmoshin Yousef Al-Duaij; Counsellor, Abdullatif A. Al-Mawwash

Kyrgyz Republic

Embassy of Kyrgyzstan (to Canada): #705, 1511 K St. NW, **Washington** DC 20005, 202/347-3732; Fax: 202/347-3718: Email: kyrgyz@aol.com; Chargé d'Affaires, a.i., Almas Chukin

Lao People's Democratic Republic
Embassy of Laos (to Canada): 2222 - 5th. NW, **Washington** DC 20008, 212/
322-6416; Fax: 202/332-4923; Ambassador, Hiem Phommachanh; First
Secretary, Seng Soukhathivong

Republic of Latvia
Embassy of Latvia: Tower B: #208, 112 Kent St., **Ottawa** ON L1P 5P2, 613/
238-6014; Fax: 613/238-7044; Email: latvia-embassy@magmacom.com;
Consular Division: 613/238-6868; Ambassador, Dr. Georges Andrevevs;
Chargé d'Affaires, Martins Lacis

Lebanese Republic
Embassy of Lebanon: 640 Lyon St., **Ottawa** ON K1S 3Z5, 613/236-5825;
Fax: 613/232-1609; Ambassador, His Excellency Dr. Assem Salman Jaber;
Counsellor, Michel Haddad; **Outremont**: Consul General, Charbel Wehbi, 40,
ch Côte Ste Catherine, Outremont PQ H2V 2A2, 514/276-2638; Fax: 514/
276-0090

Kingdom of Lesotho
High Commission for Lesotho: 202 Clemow Ave., **Ottawa** ON K1S 2B4,
613/236-9449; Fax: 613/238-3341; High Commissioner, Dr. Gwendoline M.
Malahleha, Ph.D.; Counsellor, Boomo Frank Sofonia; **Montréal**: Hon. Consul
General, Louis D. Burke, 4750, The Boulevard, Montréal PQ H3Y 1V3, 514/
482-6568; Fax: 514/483-6595; **Vancouver**: Hon. Consul, Kenneth L. Burke,

2146 - 14 Ave. West, Vancouver BC V6J 2K4, 604/734-2729; Fax: 604/734-0627

Republic of Liberia

Embassy of Liberia: Ottawa ON; **Burlington**: Hon. Consul, Edward A. Collis, 1441 Ontario St., Burlington ON L7S 1G5, 905/333-4000; Fax: 905/632-4000; **Montréal**: Hon. Consul General, H.J.F. Bloomfield, #1720, 1080 Beaver Hall Hill, Montréal PQ H2Z 1S8, 514/871-4741; Fax: 514/397-0816; **Ste-Foy**: Hon. Consul General, Erwin Singer, Toronto ON; Hon. Consul, Philip Berlach, 400, rue Morse, Ste-Foy PQ G1N 4L4; **Vancouver**: Hon. Consul General, Philip Garratt, #503, 815 Hornby St., Vancouver BC V6Z 2E6, 614/684-5988; Fax: 604/684-0367; Embassy temporarily closed

Socialist People's Libyan Arab Jamahiriya

c/o Permanent Mission of Libya to the U.N.: #309, 315 East 48th St., **New York** NY 10017, 212/752-5775; Fax: 212/593-4787; Ambassador His Excellency Mohamed Azwai; Chargé d'Affaires, Ibrahim A. Omar

Liechtenstein *c/o* Swiss Confederation

Republic of Lithuania

Embassy of Lithuania (to Canada): 2622 - 16th St. NW, **Washington** DC 20009, 202/234-5860; Fax: 202/328-0460; Ambassador designate, A. Eidintas; **Toronto**: Hon. Consul General of Lithuania, Haris Lapas, Toronto, 416/538-2992

Grand Duchy of Luxembourg
Embassy of Luxembourg (to Canada): 2200 Massachusetts Ave. NW, **Washington** DC 20008, 202/265-4171; Fax: 202/328-8270; Ambassador, His Excellency Alphonse Berns; Minister-Counsellor, Jean-Paul Munchen; **Calgary**: Hon. Consul, A.G. (Dan) Havlena, c/o Cec Papke Sales & Rentals Ltd., #216, 816 - 7 Ave. SW, Calgary AB T2P 1A1, 403/262-5576; Fax: 403/262-3556; **Montréal**: Hon. Consul General, Marie-Claire Lefort, 3877 Draper Ave., Montréal PQ H4A 2N9, 514/489-6052; **Vancouver**: Hon. Consul, Klaus Priebe, #300, 1111 Melville St., Vancouver BC V6E 4H7, 604/682-3664; Fax: 604/688-3830

Republic of Madagascar
Embassy of Madagascar: 282 Somerset St. West, **Ottawa** ON K2P 0J6, 613/563-2506; Fax: 613/231-3261; Ambassador, His Excellency René Fidèle Rajaonah; **Brossard**: Hon. Vice Consul, Julien Randrianarivony, 8520, rue Saguenay, Brossard PQ J4X 1M6, 514/672-0353; Fax: 514/466-1552; **Calgary**: Hon. Consul, Zdenek Geoffrey Havlena, c/o Cec Papke Sales & Rentals Ltd., #216, 816 -7 Ave. SW, Calgary AB T2P 1A1, 403/262-5576; Fax: 403/262-3556

Republic of Malawi
High Commission for Malawi: 7 Clemow Ave., **Ottawa** ON K1S 2A9, 613/236-8931; Fax: 613/236-1054; High Commissioner, His Excellency Emmanuel C.R. Gondwe; First Secretary, David Ntonya; **St-Lambert**: Hon. Consul, Yvon Maloney, 5437, boul Plamondon, St-Lambert PQ J4S 1W4,

514/466-9543; Toronto: Hon. Consul, Robert A. Elek, #544, 21 Dale Ave., Toronto ON M4W 1K3, 416/234-9333

Malaysia

High Commission of Malaysia: 60 Boteler St., **Ottawa** ON K1N 8Y7, 613/241-5182; Fax: 613/241-5214; Telex: 053-3520; High Commissioner, His Excellency Dato Abdullah Zawawi Bin Haji Mohamed; Counsellor, Saipul Anuar Bin Abd Muin; **Toronto**: Consul, Sahban Bin Haji Muksan, #1110, 150 York St., Toronto ON M5H 3S5, 416/947-0004; Fax: 416/947-0006; **Vancouver**: Consul General, Ali Bin Abdullah, #1900 , 925 Georgia St. West, Vancouver BC V6C 3L2, 614/685-9550; Fax: 604/685-9520

Republic of Mali

Embassy of Mali: 50 Goulburn Ave., **Ottawa** ON K1N 8C8, 613/232-1501; Fax: 613/232-7429; Ambassador, His Excellency Diakité manassa Danioko; Counsellor, Mohamed Maiga; **Montréal**: Hon. Consul, Paul Fortin, #1810, 1 Westmount Sq., Montréal PQ H3Z 2P9, 514/939-1254; Fax: 514/489-0379; **Toronto**: Hon. General Consul, Paul John Tuz, 519 Spadina Rd., Toronto ON M5P 2W6, 416/489-4849; Fax: 416/766-1970

Malta

High Commission for Malta (to Canada): c/o Embassy of Malta; 2017 Connecticut Ave. NW, **Washington** DC 20008, 202/462-3611; Fax: 202/387-5470; Email: 102475.2476@compuserve.com: Telex: 64231 MALTAREP;

High Commissioner, His Excellency Dr. Albert Borg Olivier de Puget;
Etobicoke: Hon. Consul General, Milo Vassallo, West Tower, Mutual Group
Centre, #730, 3300 Bloor St. West, Etobicoke ON M8X 2X2, 416/207-0922;
Fax: 416/207-0986; **Montréal**: Hon. Consul, Edward G. Abela, 3461
Northcliffe, Montréal PQ H4A 3K8, 514/284-3627; Fax: 514/284-1860; **St.
John's**: Hon. Consul General, Charles E. Puglisevich, Crosbie Bldg., PO Box
186, Stn C, St. John's NF A1C 5J2, 709/722-2744; Fax: 709/722-3208; **Van-
couver**: Hon. Consul General, Joachim Grubner, #310, 1001 Broadway West,
Vancouver BC V6H 4B1, 614/732-4453; Fax: 604/738-4796

Islamic Republic Mauritania
Embassy of Mauritania: 249 McLeod St., Ottawa ON K2P 1A1, 613/237-
3283; Fax: 613/237-3287; Ambassador, His Excellency Abdel Majid Kamil;
Counsellor, Sidi Ould Mohamed Lagdhaf

Republic of Mauritius
High Commission for Mauritius (to Canada): c/o Embassy of Mauritius:
#441, 4301 Connecticut Ave. NW, **Washington** DC 20008, 202/244-1491;
Fax: 202/Gervais, #200, 60 rue Cathcart, Montréal PQ H3B 1K9, 514/393-
9500; Fax: 514/393-9324

Embassy of Myanmar
#902, 85 Range Rd., **Ottawa** ON K1N 8J6, 613/232-6434; Fax: 613/232-
6435; Ambassador, His Excellency Dr. Kyaw Winung

Republic of Namibia

High Commission for Namibia (to Canada): 1605 New Hampshire Ave. NW, **Washington** DC 20009, 202/986-0540; Fax: 202/986-0443; High Commissioner, His Excellency Tuliameni Kalomoh; **Waterloo**: Hon. Consul, Walter McLean, 122 Avondale Ave. South, Waterloo ON N2L 2G3, 51978-5932; Fax: 519/578-7799

Kingdom of Nepal

Royal Nepalese Embassy (to Canada): c/o Embassy of Nepal, 2131 Leroy Place NW, **Washington** DC 20008, 202/667-4550; Fax: 202/667-5534; Telex 440085 EVER UI; Ambassador, Vacant; Chargé d'Affaires, Pradep Khapitwada; **Toronto**: Hon. Consul General, Kunjar Sharma, BDO Dunwoody Ward Mallette, Royal Bank Plaza, PO Box 33, Toronto ON M5J 2J9, 416/865-0210; Fax: 416/865-0904

Kingdom of the Netherlands

Royal Netherlands Embassy: #2020, 350 Albert St., **Ottawa** ON K1R 1A4, 613237-5030; Fax: 613/237-6471; Ambassador, His Excellency Johannes H.W. Fietelaars; Counsellor & Deputy Head of Mission, Arend H. Huitzing; Counsellor, Economic & Commercial Affairs, Aart Jan M. Verdegaal; **Calgary**: Hon. Consul, G.A. Van Wielingen, Canada Trust Tower, #2103, 421 - 7 Ave. SW, Calgary AB T2P 4K9, 403/266-2710; Fax: 403/265-8180; **Edmonton**: Hon. Consul, R. Dootjes, 10214 - 112 St., Edmonton AB T5K 1M5, 403428-7513; Fax: 403/424-2053; **Halifax**: Hon. Consul, Gavin Joseph Rainnie, Purdy's Wharf, #1306, 1959 Upper Water St., Halifax NS B3J 3N2,

902/422-1485; Fax: 902/420-1787; **Kingston**: Hon. Vice Consul, Dr. H. Westenberg, 115 Lower Union St., Kingston ON K7L 2N3, 613/542-7095; **London**: Hon. Vice Consul, Dr. R.D. ter-Vrugt, 650 Colborne St., London ON N5A 5A1, 519/551-0453; Fax: 519/432-7431; **Montréal**: Consul General, Hans van Dam, #1500, 1245, rue Sherbrooke ouest, Montréal PQ H3G 1G2, 514/849-4347; Fax: 514/849-8260; **Québec**: Hon. Consul, E.A. Price, 10, rue Ate-Anne, PO Box 833, Québec PQ G1R 3X1, 418/692-2175; Fax: 418/692-4161; **Regina**: Hon. Consul, W.B.C. de Lint, #100, 2400 College Ave., Regina SK S4P 1C8, 306/522-8577; **Saint John**: Hon. Consul, C.D. Whelly, #1600, 1 Brunswick Sq., PO Box 1324, Stn A, Saint John NB E2L 4H8, 506/632-8900; Fax: 506/632-8809; Telex: 014-47252; **St. John's**: Hon. Consul, A.A. Bruneau, 55 Kenmount Rd., PO Box 8910, St. John's NF A1B 3P6, 709737-5616; Fax: 709/737-5832; **Thunder Bay**: Hon. Vice Consul, R.P. Welter, 179 South Algoma St., Thunder Bay ON P7B 3C1, 807/344-5721; **Toronto**: Consul General, P.W.A. Schellekeus, #2106, 1 Dudnas St., West, Toronto ON M5G 1Z3, 416/598-2520; Fax: 416/589-8064; **Vancouver**: Consul General, Baron M. Van Aerssen Beijeren Van Voshol, Crown Trust Bldg., #821, 475 Howe St., Vancouver BC V6C 2B3, 604/684-6448; Fax: 604/684-3549; **Winnipeg**: Hon. Consul, Hans Hasenack, 69 Shorecrest Dr., Winnipeg MB R3P 1N9, 204/489-0467; Fax: 204-489-4219

New Zealand

New Zealand High Commission: # 727, 99 Bank St., **Ottawa** ON K1P 6G3, 613/238-5991; Fax: 613/238-5707; High Commissioner, The Hon. Stephen

Jacobs; Deputy High Commissioner, Craig A. Rickit; First Secretary, Barbara Bridge; **Vancouver**: Consul General & Trade Commissioner, Stephen Bryant, #1200, 888 Dunsmuir St., Vancouver BC V6C 3K4, 604/684-7388; Fax: 604/684-7333

Republic of Nicaragua

Embassy of Nicaragua: #407, 130 Albert St., **Ottawa** ON K1P 5G4; 613/234-9361; Fax: 613/238-7666; Consular Section: 613/238-7677; Ambassador, His Excellency Dr. René Sandino Arguello; Minister-Counsellor Chargé d'Affaires, A.I., Susan Grigsby de Fonseca; First Secretary, Consular Affairs, Juan Manuel Siero Cantarero; **Laval**: Consul, Noel Lacayo Barreto, 495 Josiane, Laval PQ H7P 5R1, 514/484-9694; Fax: 514/625-5132; **Toronto**: Hon. Consul Ilse Mendieta de McGrath, 2351 Poplar Cr., Toronto ON L5J 4H2, 905/855-3960; Fax: 905/855-1513

Republic of Niger

Embassy of Niger: 38 Blackburn Ave., **Ottawa** ON K1N 8A2, 613/232-4291; Fax: 513/230-9808; Ambassador, His Excellency Aboubacar Abdou; Counsellor, Boubacar Adarnor; Second Secretary, M. Saley Brah; **Montréal**: Hon. Consul, Pierre Thomas, #850, 231, rue St-Jacques ouest, Montréal PQ H2Y 1M6, 514/844-4428; **Toronto**: Hon Consul, Jean Michel Beck, Toronto ON; Vancouver: Hon. Consul, John Akerley, Vancouver BC

Federal Republic of Nigeria

High Commission for Nigeria: 295 Metcalfe St., **Ottawa** ON K2P 1R9, 613/

236-0521; Fax: 513/236-0529; High Commissioner, vacant; Minister-Counsellor & Acting High Commissioner, M.A.B. Adeyanju

Kingdom of Norway
Royal Norwegian Embassy: #532, 90 Sparks St., **Ottawa** ON K1P 5B4, 613/
238-6571; Fax: 613/238-2765; Ambassador, His Excellency Bjorn Inge
Kristvik; Attaché, Elna Verheyleweghen; **Calgary**: Hon. Consul, L.E.
Bjornsen, North Tower, Western Canadian Place, #1753, 707 - 8th Ave., SW,
PO Box 6525, Stn D, Calgary AB T2P 3G7, 403/263-2270; Fax: 403/298-
6081; **Darmouth**: Hon. Consul, Steinar J. Engeset, #206, 11 Morris Dr.,
Darmouth NS B3B 1M2, 902/468-1330; Fax: 902/468-7200; **Edmonton**: Hon.
Consul, roar Tungland, 2310 - 80 Ave., PO Box 5584, Edmonton AB T6C
4E9, 403/440-2292; Fax: 403/440-1241; **Mississauga**: Hon. Consul General,
Trygve Husebye, 2600 South Sheridan Way, Mississauga ON L5J 2M4, 905/
822-2339; Fax: 905/855-1450; **Montréal**: Hon. Consul General, Richard
Pound, #3900, 1155, boul René Lévesque ouest, Montréal PQ H3B 3V2, 514/
874-9087; Fax: 514/397-3063; **Québec**: Hon. kConsul, Gaétan Thivierge, 2
Nouvelle France, Wolves Crove, PO Box 40, Stn B, Québec PQ G1K 7A2,
418-525-8171; Fax: 418/525-9940; **Regina**: Hon Consul, John T. Nilson,
McCallum Hill Center, #1500, 1874 Scarth St., Regina SK S4P 4E9, 306/
347-8000; Fax: 306/352-5250; **Saint John**: Hon. Consul, Donald F.
MacGowan, Q.C., 40 Wellington Row, PO Box 6850, Stn A, Saint John NB
E2L 4S3, 506/633-3800; Fax: 506/633-3811; **St. John's**: Hon. Consul, Robert
I. Collingwood, Baine Johnston Centre, #800, 10 Fort William Place, PO Box
5367, St. John's NF A1C 5W2, 709/576-1780; Fax: 709/576-1273; **Vancou-**

ver: Hon. Consul General, Bjorn Hareid, Waterfron Centre, #1200, 200 Burrard St., Vancouver BC V6C 3L6, 604/682-7977; Fax: 604/682-8376; **Victoria**: Consul, Cecil P. Ridout, Hartwig Court, #410, 1208 Wharf St., PO Box 577, Victoria BC V8W 2P5, 250/384-1174; Fax: 250/382-3231; **Ville la Baie**: Hon. Consul, C.J. Trembray, 1522 - 6e av, Ville de la Baie PQ G7B 1R6, 418/544-1488; **Winnipeg**: Hon. Consul, Astrid Walker, 336 Lindenwood Dr. East, Winnipeg MB R3P 2H1, 204/489-1626

Sultanate of Oman
Embassy of Oman (to Canada): 2342 Massachusetts Ave. NW, **Washington** DC 20008, 202/387-1980; Fax: 202/745-4933; Ambassador, His Excellency Awadh Bader Al-Shanfari

Islamic Republic of Pakistan
High Commission for Pakistan: #608, 151 Slater St., **Ottawa** ON K1P 5H3, 613/238-7881; Fax: 613/238-7296; Email: hcpak@magi.com; High Commissioner, Farouk A. Rana; First Secretary/Head of Chancery, Muhammad Sarfraz A. Kahnzada; **Montréal**: Consul General, Muhammad Ashraf, 3421, rue Peel, Montréal PQ H3A 1W7, 514/845-2297; Fax: 514/845-1354; Telex: 033-62154; **Wilowdale**: Consul General, Yusuf Shah, #810, 4881 Yonge St., Willowdale ON M2N 5X3, 416/250-1255; Fax: 416/250-1321

Republic of Panama
Embassy of Panama (to Canada): 2862 McGill Terrace NW, **Washington** DC 20008, 202/483-1407; Fax: 202/483-8413; Ambassador, His Excellency

Ricardo Alberto Arias; **Montréal**: Consul General, Luis E. Uribe, #904, 1425, boul René Lévesque ouest, Nun's Island, Montréal PQ H3G 1T7, 514/874-1929; Vancouver: Hon. Consul, Dr. John Stuart Gladwell, #700, 555 West Hastings St., Vancouver BC V6B 4N5, 6040/893-7033; Fax: 604/687-2043

Papua New Guinea
Embassy of Papua New Guinea: #300, 1615 New Hampshire Ave., **Washington** DC 20009, 202/745-3680; Fax: 202/743-3679; Ambassador, His Excellency Nagora Bogan; **Toronto**: Hon. Consul, David Beatty, Old Canada Investment Corp. Ltd., #2700, 145 King St. West, Toronto ON M5H 1J8, 416/865-0470

Republic of Paraguay
Embassy of Paraguay: #401, 151 Slater St., **Ottawa** ON K1P 5H3, 613/567-1283; Fax: 613/567-1679; Ambassador, Washington Ashwell; First Secretary, Marta Elvira Marsiaj; **Montréal**: Hon. Consul, Claude J.Y. Le Gris, #2820, 1, Place Ville Marie, Montréal PQ H3B 4R4, 514/398-0465; Fax: 514/487-0188

Republic of Peru
Embassy of Peru: #1901, 130 Albert St., **Ottawa** ON K1P 5G4, 613/238-1777; Fax: 613/232-3062; Email: emperuca@magi.com; Telex: 052-3754 LEPRU OTT; Ambassador, His Excellency Hernan Couturier Mariategui; **Montréal**: Consul General, Raul A. Rivera Maravi, La Tour Ouest, #376, 550, rue Sherbrooke ouest, Montréal PQ H3A 1B9, 514/844-5123; Fax: 514/843-8425; **Toronto**: Consul General, Dora Salazar-Watkins, #301, 10 Saint

Mary St., Toronto ON M4Y 1P9, 416/963-9696; Fax: 416/963-9074; **Vancouver**: Consul, Amador Velasquez, #1850, 505 Burrard St., Vancouver BC V7X 1M6, 604/662-8880; Fax: 604/662-3564

Republic of the Philippines
Embassy of the Philippines: #606-608, 130 Albert St., **Ottawa** ON K1P 5G4, 613/233-1121; Fax: 613/233-4165; Ambassador, His Excellency Pacifico A. Castro; Minister-Counsellor & Consul General, Antonio P. Villamayor; **Edmonton**: Hon. Consul, Victoriano K. Cui, 8458 - 182 St., Edmonton AB T5T 2Y7, 403/444-5743; **Saint-Laurent**: Hon. Consul General, Jose M. Reyes, #202, 3300 Côte Vertu, Saint-Laurent PQ H4R 2B7, 514/335-0478; Fax: 514/335-2786; **Toronto**: Consul General, Clemencio F. Montesa, #365, 151 Bloor St. West, Toronto ON M5S 1S4, 416/922-7181; Fax: 416/922-2638; Trade Section: #409, 60 Bloor St. West, Toronto ON M42 3B8, 416/967-1788; Fax: 416/967-6236; **Vancouver**: Consul General, Lourdes G. Morales, #301-308, 470 Granville St., Vancouver BC V6C 1V5, 604/684-7645; Fax: 604/685-9945; Telex: 04-51390; **Winnipeg**: Hon. Consul, Dr. Rolando D. Guzman, 714 Medical Arts Bldg., #708, 233 Kennedy St., Winnipeg MB R3C 3J5, 204/942-7870

Republic of Poland
Embassy of Poland: 443 Daly Ave., **Ottawa** ON K1N 6H3, 613/789-0468; Fax: 613/789-1218; Email: aj201@freenet.carleton.ca; Ambassador, His Excellency Tadeusz Diem; Counsellor, Maksymilian Podstawski; **Montréal**: Consul General, Malgorzata Dzieduszycka-Ziemilska, 1500, av Pine ouest,

Montréal PQ H3G 1B4, 514/937-9481; Fax: 514/937-7272; Commercial Section: 3501, av Musée, Montréal PQ H3G 2C8, 514/937-9481; Fax: 514/937-7272; **Toronto**: Consul General, Wojciech Tycinski, 2603 Lake Shore Blvd. West, Toronto ON M8V 1G5, 416/252-5471; Fax: 41652-0509; Commercial Section: #2860, 3300 Bloor St. West, Centre Tower, Toronto ON M8X 2W8, 416/233-6571; Fax: 416/233-9578; **Vancouver**: Consul General, Krzysztof Kasprzyk, #1600, 1177 Hastings St. West, Vancouver BC V6E 2KE, 614/588-3430; Fax: 614/688-3537

Portugal
Embassy of Portugal: 645 Island Park Dr., **Ottawa** ON K1Y 0B8, 613/729-4236; Consular Section: Tel: 613/729-2270; Ambassador, His Excellency Fernando Manuel da Silva Marques; Counsellor, Vera Maria Fernandes; **Edmonton**: Hon. Consul, Luis Filipe da Rocha Rodrigues Freire, 398 Clearview Rd., Edmonton AB T5A 4G6, 403/473-1005; Fax: 403/473-2985; **Halifax**: Hon. Consul, Arthur R. Moreira, 1646 Barrington St., PO Box 355, Halifax NS B3J N27; 902/423-7211; **Montréal**: Consul General, Antonio Jorge Jacob de Carvalho, #1725, 2020, rue University, Montréal PQ H3A 2A5, 51499-0359; Fax: 51499-0366; Commercial Section: #940, 500, rue Sherbrooke ouest, Montréal PQ H3A 3C6, 514/282-1264; Fax: 514/499-1450; **Québec**: Hon. Consul, Fernao Mendonça Perestrelo, #710, 775, av Murray, Québec PQ G1S 4T2, 418/681-8650; St. John's: Hon. Consul, Hernani Eurico da Silva Martins, 40 Mansfield Cres., PO Box 5249, St. John's NF A1E 5A8, 709/726-2440, 745-2271; **Toronto**: Consul General, José Manuel da

Encarnaçao Pessanha Vieigas, 121 Richmond St. West, 7th Fl., Toronto ON M5H 2K1, 416/921-7925; Fax: 416/921-1353; **Vancouver**: Consul, Walid Maciel Chaves Saad, #904, 7009 West Pender St., Vancouver BCV6C 1G8, 604/688-6514; Fax: 604/685-7042; **Winnipeg**: Consul, Gustavo Uriel da Roza, Jr., #908, 167 Lombard Ave., Winnipeg MB R3B 1N7, 204/943-8941

State of Qatar
Embassy of Qatar (to Canada): c/o Mission to theUnited Nations: #1180, 600 New Hampshire Ave. NW, Washington DC 20037; 202/338-0111; Fax: 202/337-2989; Ambassador, His Excellency Sheikh Abdulrahman bin Saud al-Thani

Republic of Romania
Embassy of Romania: 655 Rideau St., Ottawa ON K1N 6A3, 613/789-3709; Fax: 613/789-4365; Ambassador, His Excellency Valeriu Eugen Pop; Chargé d'Affairs, Adrian Petrescu; Minister-Counsellor, Economic Affairs, Viorel One; Montréal: Consul General, Romulus-Patrus Bena, #M01.94, 1111, rue St. Urbain, Montréal PQ H2Z 1X6, 514/876-1792; Fax: 514/876-1797; **Toronto**: Consul General, Ilie Puscas, #530, 111 Peter St., Toronto ON M5V 2H1, 416/585-5802; Fax: 416/585-4798

Russian Federation
Embassy of the Russian Federation: 285 Charlotte St., **Ottawa** ON K1N 8L5, 613/235-4341; Fax: 613/236-6342; Consular Section: 52 Range Rd., Ottawa ON K1N 8J5, 613/236-7220; Fax: 613/238-6158; Ambassador, His

Excellency Alexander M. Belonogov; Minister-Counsellor, Vassili D. Sredin; Counsellor, Commercial, Valeri Makharadze; Counsellor, Consular, Vladimir Shillin; **Montréal**: Consul General, Nikoli Smirnov, 3685, av du Musée, Montréal PQ H3G 2E1, 514/843-5901; Fax: 514/942-2012; Trade Section: 95 Wurtemburg St., Ottawa ON K1N 8Z7, 613/236-1222; Fax: 612/238-2951

Rwandese Republic
121 Sherwood Dr., **Ottawa** ON K1Y 3V1, 613/722-5825; Fax: 613/729-3291; Ambassador, His Excellency Maximin Mazimpaka Segasayo; Counsellor, Faustin Kanyamibwa; **Montréal**: Hon. Consul General, Pierre Valcour, 1600 Delorimier St., Montréal PQ H2K 3W5, 514/526-1392; Fax: 514/421-7081; **North York**: Hon. Consul, Ronald Heynneman, #102, 211 Consumers St., North York ON M2J 4G8, 416/793-5474; Fax: 416/493-8171

Saint Kitts & Nevis *c/o* Organization of the Eastern Caribbean States
Halifax: Hon. Consul, E. Anthony Ross, CLL Group Building, #602, 2695 Dutch Village Rd., Halifax NS B3L 4T9, 902/455-9090

Saint Lucia *c/o* Organization of the Eastern Caribbean States
Markham: Consul, Dunstan Fontenelle, 3 Dewberry Dr., Markham ON L3S 2R7, 416/472-1423; Fax: 416/472-6379

Saint Vincent & the Grenadines *c/o* Organization of the Eastern Caribbean States; **North York**: Consul for Saint Vincent & the Grenadines, Burns

Bonadie, 210 Sheppard Ave. East, Ground Fl., North York ON M2N 3A9, 416/222-0745; Fax: 516/222-3830

San Marino

Montréal: Hon. Consul General, Raymond Lette, 27, av McNider, Montréal PQ H2V 3X4, 514/871-3838; Fax: 514/876-4217; **Toronto**: Hon. Consul, Germano Valle, #1104, 14 McMurrich St., Toronto ON M5R 3M6, 416/925-7777, 971-4848; Fax: 416/964-8937

Democratic Republic of Sao Tomé & Principe

c/o Permanent Mission of Sao Tomé & Principe to the U.N.; #1604, 122 East 42nd St., **New York** NY 10168; First Secretary, Domingos Ferreira; Montréal: Hon. Consul, Alain Berranger, 4068, av Beaconsfield, Montréal PQ H4A 2H3

Kingdom of Saudi Arabia

Royal Embassy of Saudi Arabia: #901, 99 Bank St., Ottawa ON K1P 6B9, 613/237-4100; Fax: 613/237-0567; Telex: 053-4285; Consular Section: 613/237-4104; Ambassador, His Excellency Asaad Al-Zuhair; First Secretary, Ghazi Hassad Eid

Republic of Senegal

Embassy of Senegal: 57 Marlborough Ave., Ottawa ON K1N 8E8, 613/238-6392; Fax: 613/238-2695; Counsellor, Alioune Diagne; Ambassador, His Excellency Pierre Diouf; Montréal: Hon. Consul, Louis-Philippe Lavoie,

3700, rue St-Christophe, Montréal PQ H2L 3X5, 514/526-8183; **North York**: Hon. Consul, Dr. Gérard Bastien, 2472 Bayview Ave., North York ON M2L 1A7, 416/444-7492; **Vancouver**: Hon. Consul, Kenneth John Bodnarchuk, 320 Industrial Ave., Vancouver BC V6A 2P5, 604/682-2121

Serbia *c/o* Federal Republic of Yugoslavia

Republic of Seychelles
High Commission for Seychelles (to Canada): #900$, 820 Second Ave., **New York** NY 10017 212/678-9766; Fax: 212/808-4975; High Commissioner, His Excellency Marc Marengo; Commercial Section: 1801, 275 Slater St., Ottawa ON K1P 2H9, 613/238-4002; Fax: 613/238-6226; Ambassador, His Excellency Virasakdi Futrakul; Minister, Cholchineepan Chiranond; Minister-Counsellor, Commercial, Vira Boonsri; **Edmonton**: Hon. Consul, Kurt Beier, 8625 - 112 St., Edmonton AB T6G 1K8, 403/469-3576; Fax: 403/432-1387; **Montréal**: Hon. Consul General, Marc J. Besso, #1500, 666, rue Sherbrooke ouest, Montréal PQ H3A 1E7, 514/982-0777; Fax: 514/282-7435; **Toronto**: Hon. Consul General, Richard C. Meech, Q.C., 44th Fl., Scotia Plaza, 40 King St. West, Toronto ON M5H 3Y4, 416/367-6750; Fax: 416/367-6749; Telex: 06-22687; **Vancouver**: Hon. Consul General, Horst G.P. Koehler, C.M., #106, 736 Granville St., Vancouver BC V6Z 1G3, 604/687-1143; Fax: 604/687-4434

Republic of Togo
Embassy of Togo: 12 Range Rd., **Ottawa** ON K1N 8J3, 613/238-5916, 5917;

Fax: 613/235-6425; Telex: 053-4564 AMBATOGO OTT; Ambassador, His Excellency Kossivi Osseyi; First Secretary, Economic and Commercial, Hodgo Biam; **Calgary**: Hon. Consul, Garry Tarrant, #700, 1207 - 11 Ave., Calgary AB T3C 0M5, 403/229-0103; Fax: 403/245-5156; **Toronto**: Hon. Consul, Paul John Tuz, #403, 1 St. Johns Rd., Toronto ON M6P 4C7, 416/766-5744; Fax: 416/766-1970; **Verdun**: Hon. Consul, Gérard Shanks, Verdun Consulate, 484 - 5 Ave., Verdun PQ H4G 2K1, 514/769-4888

Republic of Trinidad & Tobago

High Commission for Trinidad & Tobago: #508, 75 Albert St., Ottawa ON K1P 5E7, 613/232-2418; Fax: 613/232-4349; Email: thcotta@travel-net.com; High Commissioner, Her Excellency Shastri Ali; Deputy High Commissioner, Stephen Kangal; First Secretary, Dennison Webster; **North York**: Consul General, Cyril Blanchfield, #303, 2005 Sheppard Ave. East, North York ON M2J 5B4, 416/495-9442; Fax: 416/495-6934

Republic Tunisia

Embassy of Tunisia: 515 O'Connor St., Ottawa ON K1S 3P8; 613/237-0330; Fax: 513/237-7939; Ambassador, His Excellency Khalifa El Hafdhi; **Montréal**: Consul, Hachem Ben Achour, #600, 511, Place d'Armes, Montréal PQ H2Y 2W7, 514/289-8633; Fax: 514/288-6469

Republic of Turkey

Embassy of Turkey: 197 Wurtemburg St., Ottawa ON K1N 8L9, 613/789-4044; Fax: 613/789-3442; Ambassador, His Excellency Omer Ersun; Coun-

sellor, Hasan Servet Oktem; Counsellor, Economic & Commercial, Erdogan
Hurbas; **Montréal**: Hon. Consul General, Ali T. Argun, #2500, 1100, boul
René-Lévesque ouest, Montéal PQ H3B 5C9, 514/397-6903; Fax: 514/397-
5815

Republic of Uganda

High Commission for Uganda: 231 Cobourg St., Ottawa ON K1N 8J2, 612/
789-7797; Fax: 613/789-8909; Telex: 053-4469; High Commissioner, His
Excellency Dr. Tibamanya mewene Mushanga; Counsellor, James H.O.
Okullo

Republic of Ukraine

Embassy of Ukraine: 310 Somerset St. West, Ottawa ON K2P 0J9, 513/230-
2961; Fax: 613/230-2400; Consular Section: 613/230-8015; Ambassador, His
Excellency Volodymyz Furkalo; Commissioner, Trade, Igor Sanin

United Arab Emirates

c/o Permanent Mission of the United Arab Emirates to the U.N.: 747
Third Ave., **New York** NY 10017, 212/371-0480; Fax: 212/371-4923; Ambas-
sador, His Excellency Mohammed J. Samhan; First Secretary, Khalid K. Al-
Mualla; First Secretary, Yacub Y. Al-Hosani; Third Secretary, Omar S.
Ghobash

United Kingdom of Great Britain & Northern Ireland

British High Commission: 80 Elgin St., **Ottawa** ON K1P 5K7, 613/237-

1530; Fax: 9613/237-7980; High Commissioner, His Excellency Anthony M. Goodenough, K.C.M.G.; Deputy High Commissioner, Linda Duffield; Counsellor, Economic & Commercial, Boyd McCleary; Counsellor, Robert M.F. Kelly; **Dartmouth**: Hon. L. Staughan, 1 Canal St., PO Box 605, Stn M. Dartmouth NS B2Y 3YB, 902/422-0313; Fax: 902/463-7678; **Montréal**: Consul General, I. Rawlinson, #4200, 1000, rue de la Gauchetière ouest, Montréal PQ H3B 4W5, 514/866-5863; Fax: 514/866-0202; **St. John's**: Hon. Consul, Frank D. Smith, 113 Topsail Rd., St. John's NF A1E 2A9, 709/679-2002; Fax: 709/579-0475; **Toronto**: Consul General, Peter D.R. Davies, College Park, #2800, 777 Bay St., Toronto ON M5G 2G2, 416/593-1290; Fax: 416/593-1229; **Vancouver**: Consul General, B.P. Austin, #800, 1111 Melville St., Vancouver BC V6E 3V6, 604/683-4421; Fax: 604/681-0693; **Winnipeg**: Hon. Consul, R.E.M. Hill, 229 Athlone Dr., Winnipeg MB R3J 3L6, 204/896-1380; Fax: 204/896-3025

United States of America
Embassy of U.S.A.: 100 Wellington St., PO Box 866, Stn B. **Ottawa** ON K1P 5T1, 613/238-5335; Fax: 613/238-8750; Consular Section: 85 Albert St., Ottawa ON K1P 6A4, 613/238-5335; Ambassador, The Hon. James J. Blanchard; Minister, The Hon. James Walsh; Minister-Counsellor, Economic Affairs, Marshall Casse; Minister-Counsellor, Environment, Science & Technological Affairs, Thomas J. Wajda; **Calgary**: Consul General, William N. Witting, #1050, 615 Macleod Trail SE, Calgary AB T2G 4T8, 403/266-8962; Fax: 403/264-6630; **Halifax**: Consul General, Roger A. Meece, Scotia Square, 910 Cogswell Tower, Halifax NS B3J 3K1, 902/429-2480; Fax: 902/423-

6861; **Montréal**: Consul General, R. Susan Wood, 455 boul René Lévesque, CP 65, Stn Desjardins, Montréal PQ H2Z 1Z2, 514/398-9695; Fax: 514/398-0973; **Québec**: Consul General, Marie T. Huhtala, 2, Place Terrasse Dufferin, CP 939, Québec PQ G1R 4T9, 418/692-2095; Fax: 418/692-4640; Telex: 051-2275; **Toronto**: Consul General, G. Alfred Kennedy, 360 University Ave., Toronto ON M5G 1S4, 416/595-1700; Fax: 416/595-0051; **Vancouver**: Consul General, David T. Johnson, 1095 Pender St. West, Vancouver BC V6E 2M6, 604/685-4311; Fax: 604/685-5285

Eastern Republic of Uruguay
Embassy of Uruguay: #1905, 130 Albert St., **Ottawa** ON K1P 5G4, 613/234-2727; Fax: 613/233-4670; Email: urott@iosphere.net; Consular Section: 234-2937; Ambassador, Elbio Rosselli; First Secretary, Eduardo Anon; First Secretary, Eduardo Anon; Second Secretary, Carlos Gitto; **North York**: Hon. Consul, Carlos Garcia, #1610, 2 Sheppard Ave. East, North York ON M2N 5Y7, 416/221-7799; Fax: 416/221-7199; **Vancouver**: Hon. Consul, Conrado Beckerman, 2331 Granville St., Vancouver BC V6H 3G4, 604/739-0389; Fax: 604/731-6702

Holy See
Apostolic Nunciature: 724 Manor Ave., Rockcliffe Park, **Ottawa** ON K1M 0E3, 613/746-4914; Fax: 613/746-4786; Apostolic Nuncio, His Excellency The Most Rev. Carlo Curis; First Secretary, The Right Rev. Vito Rallo

Republic of Venezuela

Embassy of Venezuela: 32 Range Rd., **Ottawa** ON K1N 8J4, 613/235-5151; Fax: 613/746-2471; Counsellor, Marisol Black; Minister-Counsellor, Beatrice Gerbasi; Ambassador, His Excellency Felix Rossi Guerrero; **Montréal**: Consul General, Nelly Pulido de Tagliaferro, #400, 2055, rue Peel, Montréal PQ H3A 1V4, 514/842-3417; Fax: 514/287-7101; Telex: 05-267523; **Toronto**: Consul General, Hilda Hernandez, #1904, 365 Bloor St. East, Toronto ON M4W 3L4, 416/960-6070; Fax: 416/960-6077

Socialist Republic of Viet Nam

Embassy of Vietnam: 24B Davidson Dr., Gloucester ON K1J 6L7, 613/744-4963, Consular Section 745-9735; Fax: 613/744-1709, Consular Section 744-5072; Ambassador, His Excellency Dang Nghiem Bai; Counsellor, Commercial, Tran Ve

Western Samoa

High Commission for Western Samoa (to Canada): #800D, 820 Second Ave., **New York** NY 10017, 212/599-6196; Fax: 212/599-0797; High Commissioner, His Excellency Tuiloma Neroni Slade

Republic of Yemen

Embassy of Yemen: #1100, 350 Sparks St., **Ottawa** ON K1R 7S8, 613/232-8525; Fax: 613/232-8276; Ambassador, His Excellency Dr. Mohamed Saed Ali; First Secretary, Abdullah Fadhel

Federal Republic of Yugoslavia

Embassy of Yugoslavia: 17 Blackburn Ave., **Ottawa** ON K1N 8A2, 613/233-6289; Fax: 613/233-7850; First Secretary & Chargé d'Affaires, A. Mitic; Ambassador, Vacant; **Montréal**: Hon. Consul, Kalman Samuels, 1200, rue du Fort, Montréal PQ H3H 2B3, 514/939-1200

Republic of Zaire

Embassy of Zaire: 18 Range Rd., **Ottawa** ON K1N 8J3, 613/236-7103; Fax: 613/567-1404; Telex: 053-4314; Minister-Counsellor, Kalombo Kabundi Lukusa; Ambassador, His Excellency Kaweta Milombe Sampassa; **Montréal**: Hon. Consul General, Luc-Jacques Pirard, Montréal Consulate, #504, 410, rue St-Nicola, Montréal PQ H2Y 2P5, 514/845-0271

Republic of Zambia

High Commission for Zambia: #1610, 130 Albert St., **Ottawa** ON K1P 5G4; High Commissioner, His Excellency Joshua S. Siyolwe; First Secretary, B.L. Tompwe

Republic of Zimbabwe

High Commission for the Republic of Zimbabwe: 332 Somerset St. West, **Ottawa** ON K2P 0J9, 613/237-4388; Fax: 613/563-8269; High Commissioner, Her Excellency Lillie Chitauro; Counsellor, Commercial, Wilbert C.T.T. Dumba; Counsellor, Erasmus Moyo

Canadian Diplomatic Representatives Abroad

Republic of Albania *c/o* Republic of Hungary

People's Democratic Republic of Algeria
Canadian Embassy: 27 bis, rue des Frères Benhafid, Hydra, (011-213-2) 69-16-11; Fax: (011-213-2) 69-39-20; Email: MITNET: 380-0000: Telex: 266043; (66043 CANAD DZ); Postal Address: PO Box 255, Alger-Gare, 1600 Alger, **Algeria**: Ambassador, Jacques Noiseux; Counsellor, Commercial, W.A. McKenzie; Commercial Officer, Zahra Bensalah, Email: zahra.bensalah@paris03.x400.gc.ca

Principality of Andorra *c/o* Kingdom of Spain

People's Republic of Angola *c/o* Republic of Zimbabwe
Luanda: Hon. Consul, Allan Cain, Honorary Consulate of Canada, Rua Rei Katyavala #113, Luanda, Angol, (011-244-2) 330-243; Fax: (011-244-2) 343-754 (2100-0800hrs Angola time); Telex: 0991-4072/-4073/-4081 (CIAM AN)

Angulla *c/o* Barbados

Antigua & Barbuda *c/o* Barbados

Argentine Republic
Canadian Embassy: Tagle 2828, 1425, **Buenos Aires** (011-54-1) 805-3032;

Fax: (011-54-1) 805-209; Email: MITNET: 381-0000; Postal Address: Casilla de Correo 1598, Buenos Aires, Argentina: Ambassador, Robert G. Clark; First Secretary, Commercial & Economic, S. Harper; Ambassador, Uruguay, Roland Goulet; Commercial Officer, Elena Masciarelli, Email: elena.masciarelli@bairs01.x400.gc.ca

Republic of Armenia *c/o* Russian Federation

Aurba *c/o* Republic of Venezuela

Commonwealth of Australia
Canadian High Commission: Commonwealth Ave., **Canberra** ACT 2600, (011-61-6) 273-3844; Fax: (011-61-2) 273-3285; Email: MITNET: 342-0000; High Commissioner, Brian Schumacher; Deputy High Commissioner, G.J. Wilson; Counsellor, Commercial, J.F. Donaghy; Commercial Officer, Robert G. Gow, Email: Bob.Gow@sydny01.x400.gc.ca; **Perth**: Hon. Consul, R.B. Blake, Honorary Consulate of Canada, 267 St. George's Terrace, 3rd Fl., Perth WA 6000, Australia, (011-61-09) 322-7930; **South Melbourne**: Hon. Consul, T. Moore, Honorary Consulate of Canada, DMR Bldg., Level 8, 1 Southbank Blvd., **South Melbourne** VIC 3205, Australia, (011-61-03) 645-8643; Fax: (011-61-03) 643-8647; Sydney: Consul General, Alan Virtue, Canadian Consulate General, Quay West Bldg, Level 5, 111 Harrington St., **Sydney** NSW 2000, Australia, (011-61-2) 364-3000; Fax: (011-61-2) 364-3098; Cable: CANADIAN SYDNEY; MITNET: 351-0000

Republic of Austria

Canadian Embassy: Laurenzerber 2, A-1010, Vienna (011-43-1) 531-38-3000; Fax: (011-43-1) 631-38-3321; Email: MITNET: 450-3321; Cable: DOMCAN VIENNA; Ambassador, Peter F. Walker; Counsellor, Commercial, T. Marr; Minister-Counsellor, P. McKellar; Commercial Officer, Rolan J. Rossi, Email: roland.rossi@vienn02.x400.gc.ca

Republic of Azerbaijan *c/o* Turkey

Azores *c/o* Portuguese Republic

Commonwealth of the Bahamas *c/o* Jamaica

Nassau: Hon. Consul, H.A. Jacobsen, Honorary Consulate of Canada, Shirley Street Plaza, PO Box SS-6371, Nassau, Bahamas, 809/393-2123; Fax: 809/393-1305; Telex: 20246 (BEAVER BAH)

State of Bahrain *c/o* State of Kuwait

People's Republic of Bangladesh

Canadian High Commission: House CWN 16/A, Rd. 48, Gulshan Ave., **Dhaka**, (011-880-2) 88-36-39; Fax: (011-88-2) 88-30-43; Email: MITNET: 319-0000; Cable: DOMCAN DHAKA; Postal Address: GPO Box 569, Dhaka, Bangladesh; High Commissioner, Nicholas Etheridge; Counsellor, Development, J. Deyell; Senior Commercial Officer, Syed Shamimur Rahman, Email: syed.rahman@dhaka01.x400.gc.ca

Barbados
Canadian High Commission: Bishop's Court Hill, St. Michael, 809/429-3550; Fax: 809/437-8474; Email: MITNET: 318-0000; Telex: 2247 (2247 CANADA WB); Cable: DOMCAN BRIDGETOWN; Postal Address: PO Box 404, **Bridgetown**, Barbados; High Commissioner, Colleen Swords; Counsellor, K. Harley; Counsellor, Commercial, P. Hermant; Counsellor, Development, N. Norcott; Trade /Commissioner, Peter Hermant

Republic of Belarus *c/o* Russian Federation

Kingdom of Belgium
Canadian Embassy: 2, av de Tervuren, 1040, Brussels (011-32-2) 741-0606; Fax: (011-32-2) 741-0613; Email: MITNET: 488-3211; Cable: DOMCAN BRUSSELS; Ambassador, Jean-Paul Hubert; Minister/Counsellor, G. B~échard; Counsellor, Commercial/Economic, S. Doyon; Commercial Officer, Bart Roefmans

Belize *c/o* Jamaica
Belize City: Lester Young, Hon. Consul, Honorary Consulate of Canada, 85 North Front St., PO Box 610, Belize City, Belize, (011-501-02) 33-722; Fax: (011-501-02) 30-060

Republic of Benin *c/o* Federal Republic of Nigeria

Bermuda *c/o* United States of America

Republic of Bolivia *c/o* Republic of Peru

La Paz: Hon. Consul, Hector Arduz, Honorary Consulate of Canada, Av 20 de octubre 2475, Plaza Avaroa, Sopocachi, PO Box 13045, La Paz, Bolivia, (011-591-2) 37-52-24; Fax: (011-591-2) 43-23-30

Republic of Botswana *c/o* Republic of Zimbabwe

Gaborone: Hon. Consul, D. Leonard, Honorary Consulate of Canada, PO Box 1009, Gaborone, Botswana, (011-267) 371-659

Federative Republic of Brazil

Canadian Embassy: Setor de Embaixadas Sul, #803, Ava das Naçcoes, lote 16, 70410-900, Brasilia, D.F. (011-55-61) 321-2171; Fax: (011-55-61) 321-4529; Email: MITNET: 384-0000; Postal Address: Caixa Postal 00961, 70359-900 **Brasilia** D.F., Brazil; Ambassador, Nancy M. Stiles; Counsellor & Consul, B. Wilkin; Counsellor, Commercial/Economic, P. Williams; Commercial Officer (Sao Paulo), Mariangela Olivieri de Lima, Email: td.spalo@spalo01.x400.gc.ca; Rio de Janeiro: Hon. Consul, Jack Delmar, Honorary Consulate of Canada, Rua Lauro Muller 166, #2707, Torre Rio Sul, Botafogo, 22290-160, Rio De Janeiro, Brazil, (011-55-21) 275-2195; Sap Paulo: Consul General, Michael C. Spencer, Canadian Consulate General, Edificio Top Centre, Ava Paulista 854, 5th Fl., 01310-913, Sao Paulo, Brazil, (011-55-11) 287-2122; Fax: (011-55-11) 251-5057; MITNET: 376-0000

British Virgin Islands *c/o* Barbados

Brunei
Canadian High Commission: #219, Sheraton Utama Hotel, Jalan Tasek, **Bandar Seri Begawn**, (011-673-2) 22-00-43; Fax: (011-673-2) 22-00-40; Postal Address: PO Box 2808, Bandar Seri Begawan 1028, Brunei; High Commissioner, Richard Belliveau; Counsellor, Development, M. Archambault; Counsellor, Development, T. Broughton

Republic of Bulgaria *c/o* Republic of Romania

Burkina-Faso
Canadian Embassy: Agostino Neto St., PO Box 548, **Ouagaougou**, (011-226) 31-18-94; Fax: (011-226) 31-19-00; Telex: 5264 (DOMCAN BF); Postal Address: PO Box 548, Ouagadougou 01, Kadiogo, Burkina-Faso; Ambassador, Louise Ouimet; First Secretary, Development, S. Ostiguy

Republic of Burundi *c/o* Republic of Kenya
Bujumbura: Hon. Consul, J.M.A. Persoons, Honorary Consulate of Canada, boul du 28 novembre, CP 5, Bujumbura, Burundi, (011-257) 22-16-32; Fax: (011-257) 22-28-16

Kingdom of Cambodia
Canadian Embassy: Villa II, St. 254, Chartamuk Ward, District Daun Penh,

Phnom Penh, (011-855-23) 426-000; Fax: (011-855-23) 362-429; Ambassador, Gordon Longmuir

Republic of Cameroon
Canadian Embassy: Immeuble Stamatiades, Place de l'Hˆôtel de Ville, **Yaoundé**, (011-237) 22-19-36; Fax: (011-237) 22-10-90; Email: MITNET: 317-0000; Cable: DOMCAN YAOUNDÉ; Postal Address: PO Box 572, Yaoundé, Cameroon; Ambassador, Pierre Giguère; Counsellor, Development, P. Marion

Republic of Cape Verde *c/o* Republic of Senegal

Cayman Islands *c/o* Jamaica

Central African Republic *c/o* Republic of Cameroon
Quartier Sissongo Bangui: Hon. Consul, Lyne Godmaire, Honorary Consulate of Canada, PO Box 973, Quartier Sissongo Bangui, Central African Republic

Republic of Chad *c/o* Republic of Cameroon

Republic of Chile
Canadian Embassy: Ahumada 11, 10th Fl., **Santiago** (011-56-2) 696-2256; Fax: (011-56-2) 696-2424; Email: stago.td@stago01.x400.gc.ca; MITNET: 386-0000; Telex: 240341 (DOMCAN CL); Cable: DOMCAN SANTIAGO DE CHILE; Postal Address: Casilla 427, Santiago, Chile; Ambassador, Marc

Lortie; Counsellor, Commercial, P. Furesz; Commercial Officer, Margot
Edwards; Conception: Honorary Consulate of Canada, a/s ABN AMRO Bank,
PO Box 425, Conception, Chile, Fax: (011-56-2) 696-0738

People's Republic of China
Canadian Embassy: 19 Dong Zhi Men Wai St., Chao Yang District, **Beijing**
100600, (011-86-10) 532-3536; Fax: (011-86-10) 532-4072; Email:
td.bejing@bejing03.x400.gc.ca; MITNET: 341-0000; Cable: DOMCAN
PEKING; Ambassador, Howard Balloch; Minister, Commercial, K. Sunquist;
Minister-Counsellor & Consul, G. Saint-Jacques; Third Secretary (Commer-
cial), David Murphy, Email: david.murphy@bejing03.x400.gc.ca; Commercial Officer/Interpreter, Q. Chen, Email: qi.chen@bejing0x.400.gc.ca;
Guangzhou: Consul, M.C. Boyd, Consulate of Canada, China Hotel Office
Tower, #1563-4, Liu Hua Lu, Guangzhou 510015, P.R. China, (011-86-20)
666-0569; Fax: (011-86-20) 667-2401; Shanghai: Consul General, Ted
Lipman, Canadian Consulate General, American International Centre, Shanghai Centre, West Tower, #604, 1376 Nanjing Xi Lu, Shanghai 200040, P.R.
China, (011-86-21) 6279-8400; Fax: (011-1-86-21) 6279-8401; Telex: 33608
(33608 CANAD CN)

Republic of Colombia
Canadian Embassy: Calle 76, No. 11-52, Bogota (011-57-1) 313-1355; Fax:
(011-57-1) 316-3046; Cable: CANADIAN BOGOTA; Postal Address:
Apartado Aéreo 53531, Bogotá 2, Colombia; Ambassador, C. William Ross;
Counsellor, Commercial, Z.W. Burianyk; Counsellor & Consul, D. Gillett;

Commercial Officer, Carlos E. Rivera, Email: carlos.rivera@bgota01.x400.gc.ca

Islamic Federal Republic of the Comoros *c/o* United Republic of Tanzania

People's Republic of the Congo *c/o* Republic of Zaire

Republic of Costa Rica
Canadian Embassy: Apartado Postal 351-1007, San José, (011-506) 296-4149; Fax: (011-506) 296-4270; Email: MITNET: 388-0000; Ambassador, Dan Goodleaf; Counsellor & Consul, G. Lapointe; First Secretary & Consul, Commercial, M. Lebleu; Commercial Officer, Adolfo Quesada V., Email: adolfo.quesada@sjos01.x400.gc.ca

Republic of Croatia
Canadian Embassy: Hotel Esplanade: Mihanoviceva 1, 10000, Zagreb; (011-385-1) 457-7885; Fax: (011-385-1) 457-7913; Ambassador, Graham N. Green; Counsellor & Consul, Commercial, R. Lecoq

Republic of Cuba
Canadian Embassy: Calle 30, No. 518, Esquina a 7a, Miramar, **Havana**, (011-53-7) 33-25-16; Fax: (011-53-7) 33-20-44; Email: MITNET: 389-0000; Telex: 51-1586 (51-1586 CANCU); Cable: DOMCAN HAVANA; Ambassador, Mark Entwistle; Counsellor & Consul, Commercial, R. Mailhot
Varadero: Hon. Consul, Y. des Hayes, Honorary Consulate of Canada,

Granma Hotel, Bloque 18, apt. 210, Varadero, Cuba, (011-56) 64-177; Fax: (011-56) 33-7149

Republic of Cyprus *c/o* State of Israel
Nicosia: Hon. Consul, M.G. Ioannides, Honorary Consulate of Canada, Margarita House, #403, 15 Thermistocles Dervis St., **Nicosia**, Cyprus, (011-357-2) 45-16-30; Fax: (011-357-2) 45-90-96; Telex: 2110 (MARCO CY); Postal Address: PO Box 2125, Nicosia, Cyprus

Czech Republic
Canadian Embassy: Mickiewiczova 6, 135 33, Prague 6 (011-42-2) 2431-1108; Fax: (011-42-2) 2431-0294; Email: MITNET: 305-0000; Telex: 121061(911308 DMCN CH): Cable: DOMCAN PRAGUE; Ambassador, Alain Dudoit; Counsellor & Consul, Y. Jobin; Counsellor, Commercial, R. Bélanger; Commercial Officer, Pavel Szappanos, Email: pavel/szappanos@prgue01.x400.gc.ca

Kingdom of Denmark
Canadian Embassy: Dr. Bernikowsgade 1, 1105, Copenhagen K, (011-45-33) 12-22-99; Fax: (011-45-33) 12-42-10; Email: copen.td@copen.01x400.gc.ca: MITNET: 460-0000; Ambassador, Brian Baker; R.C.D., Looye, Counsellor & Consul; Counsellor, Commercial, G. Cadieux; Commercial Officer, David Horup

Republic of Djibouti *c/o* Democratic Republic of Ethiopia

Djibouti: Hon. Consul, R. Arsenault, Honorary Consulate of Canada, c/o SNC-Lavalin, House No. 233, Kampala St., PO Box 914, Djibouti, Djibouti, (011-253) 35-11-59; Fax: (011-253) 35-44-23

Commonwealth of Dominica *c/o* Barbados

Dominican Republic

Canadian Embassy: Maximo Gomez 30, **Santo Domingo**; 809/689-0002; Fax: 809/682-2691; Telex: 3460270; Postal Address: PO Box 2054, Santo Domino 1, Dominican Republic; Ambassador (resident in Caracas, Venezuela), Yves Gagnon; Counsellor & Consul, Commercial (Caracus, Venezuela), P. Giroux; First Secretary & Consul, Commercial (Caracus, Venezuela), g. Lemieux; **Puerto Plata**: Hon. Consul, T. Hall, Honorary Consulate of Canada, #3, Beller 51, Puerto Plata, Dominican Republic, 809/586-5761; Fax: 809/586-5762; Telex: 3462022

Republic of Ecuador

Edificio Josueth Gonzalez, 4th Fl., Ava, 6 de Diciembre, 2816, **Quito**, (011-593-2) 564-795; Fax: (011-593-2) 503-108; Postal Address: PO Box 17-11-6512, Quito, Ecuador; Ambassador, David Adam; Third Secretary & Consul, Administration, M. Felisiak Guayaquil; Hon. Consul, F. Costa, Honorary Consulate of Canada, Edificio Torres de la Merced, Piso 21, General Cordova 800 y Victor Manuel Rendon, Guayaquil, Ecuador, (011-593-4) 566-747; Fax: (011-593-4) 314-562; Telex: 42513

Arab Republic of Egypt

Canadian Embassy: 5 Midan El Saraya el Kobra St., **Garden City**, Cairo; (011-20-2) 354-3110; Fax: (011-21-2) 354-7549; Email: MITNET: 392-0000; Postal Address: PO Box 1667, Cairo, Egypt; Ambassador, Michael D. Bell; Counsellor & Consul, Commercial/Economic, D. Paterson; Counsellor, Development, J. Sinclair; Commercial Officer, Hany W. Ibrahim, Email: hany.h.w.i.ibrahim@cairo0l.x400.gc.ca; Alexandria: Hon. Consul, A.M.M. Khairy, Honorary Consulate of Canada, Arab Express Shipping Co., 59 El Horria St., Alexandria, Egypt, (011-50-2) 203-490-9696

Republic of El Salvador

Canadian Embassy: Ava Las Palmas no. 111, **Colonia San Benito**, San Salvador, (011-503-2) 794-655; Fax: (011-503-2) 790-765; Postal Address: Apartado Postal 3078, Centro de Gobierno, San Salvador, El Salvador; Ambassador (located in Guatamala City), James Fox; Hon. Consul, J.D. Hunter; Counsellor, Development (located in Guatamala City), E.W.E. Doe; Counsellor, development (located in Tegulcigalpa, Honduras), J. Touzel; San Salvador: Hon. Consul, James D. Hunter, Canadian Consulate, 111 Av. Las Palmas, Colonia San Benito, San Salvador, El Salvador, (011-503) 241-648; Fax: (011-503) 790-765; Postal Address: Apartado Postal 3078, Centro de Gobierno, San Salvador

Eritrea *c/o* Democratic Republic of Ethiopia
Canadian Embassy: Toom Kooli 13, 2nd. Fl., 0100, Tallinn, (011-372) 631-3570; Fax: (022-372) 631-3573; Ambassador (located in **Stockholm**, Swe-

den), William L. Clarke; Minister-Counsellor (located in Riga, Latvia), G.R. Skinner; First Secretary, Commercial (located in Latvia), H.J. Kunzer

Republic of Estonia

Canadian Embassy: Toom Kooli 13, 2nd. Fl., 0100, Tallinn, (011-372) 631-

Democratic Republic of Ethiopia

Canadian Embassy: Old Airport Area, Higher 23, Kebele 12, #122, **Addis Ababa**, (011-251-1) 71-30-22; Fax: (011-251-1) 71-30-33; Telex: 21053 (DOMCAN ET); Cable: DOMCAN ADDIS; Postal Address: PO Box 1130, Addis Ababa, Ethiopia; Ambassador, Gabriel M. Lessard; Counsellor & Consul, Development, P. Hitschfeld; First Secretary & Consul, T. Martin

European Union

The Mission of Canada to the European Union: av de Tervuren 2, 1040, **Brussels**, (011-32-2) 741-0660; Fax: (011-32-2) 741-0629; Email: MITNET: 448-3274; Head of Mission, Ambassador, Jacques Roy; Deputy Head of Mission & Minister-Counsellor, R. Hage; Counsellor, Economic Affairs, R. Stewart; Counsellor, Science & Technology, W. Coderre; Counsellor, Trade Policy, S. Brereton

Falkland Islands *c/o* Argentine Republic

Faroe Islands *c/o* Kingdom of Denmark

Fiji *c/o* New Zealand
Suva: Hon. Consul, Michael T. Brook, Honorary Consulate of Canada,
L.I.C.I. Bldg., 7th Fl, Butt St., Suva, Fiji, (011-679) 30-05-89; Fax: (011-679)
30-02-96; Postal Address: PO Box 2193, Govt. Bldg., Suva, Fiji

Republic of Finland
Canadian Embassy: P. Esplanadi 25B, 00100, **Helsinki** (011-358-0) 17-11-
41; Fax: (011-358-0) 60-10-60; Email: MITNET: 442-0000; Postal Address:
PO Box 779, 00101 Helsinki, Finland; Ambassador, Isabelle Massip; Coun-
sellor & Consul, Commercial, Leopold Battel; Commercial Officer, Risto
Pakarinen

French Republic
Canadian Embassy: 35, av Montaigne, 75008, **Paris** (011-33-1) 44-43-29-
00; Fax: (011-33-1) 44-43-29-99; Email: MITNET: 447-2900; Telex: 651806
(CANADA 280806F/CANADB 280806F); Cable: STADACONA PARIS;
Ambassador, Jacques Roy; Minister, Noble, J.J. Noble; Minister-Counsellor,
Commercial & Economic, B. Côté; Commercial Officer, Linda Bernard; La
Wantzenau: Hon. Consul, Jean-Jacques Hetzel, Honorary Consulate of
Canada, Polysar France, rue de Ried, La Wantzenau, France, (011-33) 88-96-
65-02; Fax: (011-33) 88-96-64-54; Postal Address: CP 7, 67610 La
Wantzenau, France; Lyon: Consul, Anne-Marie Viarouge-Sagala, Consulate of
Canada, Bonnel Bldg., Part-Dieu, 74, rue de Bonnel, 3e étage, 69003, **Lyon**,
France, (011-33-4) 72-61-15-25; Fax: (011-33-4) 78-62-09-36; Nice: Hon.
Consul, M. Felizzola, Honorary Consulate of Canada, c/o Agence de Voyages

French Med'Tours, 64, av Jean Médecin, 06000, Nice, France, (011-33-4) 88-96-65-02; Fax: (011-33-4) 88-96-64-54; **St. Pierre**: Hon. Consul, F. Park, Honorary Consulate of Canada, Institut Frecher, CP 903, St. Pierre, St. Pierre et Miquelon, F-97500, (508) 41-55-10; Fax: (508) 41-55-01; Toulouse: Hon. Consul, Jacques Guibert, Honorary Consulate of Canada, 30, boul de Strasbourg, 31014, Toulouse, France, (011-33-5) 51-99-30-16; Fax: (011-33-5) 61-63-43-37; Postal Address: CP 138, Toulouse, France

French Polynesia *c/o* French Republic

Gabonese Republic
Canadian Embassy: PO Boc 4037, Libreville, (011-241) 74-34-64; Fax: (011-241) 74-34-66; Email: MITNET: 326-0000; Telex: 5527 GO (DOMCAN 5527 GO); Ambassador, Louise Charron Fortin; Attaché & Consul, Administration, Y. Levesque

Republic of the Gambia *c/o* Republic of Senegal

Republic of Georgi *c/o* Republic of Turkey

Federal Republic of Germany
Canadian Embassy: Freidrich-Wilhelm-Strasse 18, 53113, **Bonn**, (011-49-228) 968-0; Fax: (011-49-228) 968-3904; Email: MITNET: 449-0000; Telex: 886421 (886421 DOMCA D); Cable: DOMCAN BONN; Ambassador, Gaétan Lavertu; Minister, L Friedlaender; Minister-Counsellor, Commercial,

Ed Mallory; Technology Development Officer, Jutta Zillgen-Schaefer; **Berlin**: Minister, Adreaan de Hoog, Canadian Embassy Office, Friedrich-Strasse 95, 10117, Berlin, Germany, (011-49-30) 261-1161; Fax: (011-49-30) 262-9206; Telex: 305099 (305099 CANAD D); Düsseldorf: Consul, R.M. Bollman, Canadian Consulate, Prinz-Georg-Strasse 126, 40479, Düsseldorf, Germany, (011-49-211) 17-21-70; Fax: (011-49-211) 35-91-65; Hamburg: Consul & Senior Trade Commissioner, D. Baker, Canadian Consulate, ABC Strasse, 45, 20534, Hamburg, Germany, (011-49-40) 255-56290; Fax: (011-49-40) 355-66294; Munich: Consul & Senior Trade Commissioner, J. Lang, Canadian consulate, Tal 29, 803331, Munich, Germany, (011-49-89) 29-06-50; Fax: (011-49-89) 228-065-199

Republic of Ghana
Canadian High Commission: 42 Independence Ave., **Accra**, (011-233-21) 77-37-91; Fax: (011-233-21) 77-37-92; Email: MITNET: 313-0000; Postal Address: PO Box 1639, Accra, Ghana; High Commissioner, John Schram; First Secretary, W. Gusen; First Secretary, Development, A. Lavender; First Secretary, Development, C. Thiruchittampalamj

Gibraltar *c/o* United Kingdom of Great Britain & Northern Ireland

Hellenic Republic
Canadian Embassy: 4 Ioannou Gennadiou St., **Athens**, (011-30-1) 725-4011; Fax: (011-30-1) 725-3994; Email: MITNET: 451-0000; Cable: DOMCAN

ATHENS; Ambassador, Derek Fraser; Counsellor, Commercial, D. Cohen; commercial Officer, Marianna Saropoulous

Greenland *c/o* Kingdom of Denmark
Nuuk: Hon. Consul, Lars Peter Danielsen, Canadian Honorary Consulate, Groenlandsfly A/S, 3900, Nuuk, Greenland, (001-299) 28888; Fax: (011-299) 27288; Telex: 90602; Postal Address: PO Box 1012, 3900 Nuuk, Greenland

Grenada *c/o* Barbados

Saint Vincent & the Grenadines *c/o* Barbados

Guadeloupe *c/o* Barbados

Guam *c/o* Japan

Republic of Guatemala
Canadian Embassy: 13 calle 8-44, Zone 10, Edyma Plaza, **Guatemala City**, (011-52-2) 33-61-04; Fax: (011-52-2) 33-61-61; Email: MITNET: 312-0000; Telex: 5206 (5206 CANADA GU); Cable: CANADIAN GUATEMALA CITY; Postal Address: PO Box 400 Guatemala City, Guatemala; Ambassador, Daniel Livermore; Counsellor & Consul, Commercial, R. Shaw-Wood; Counsellor & Consul, Development, E.W.E. Doe; Commercial Assistant, Margo Dannemiller, Email: margo.dannemiller@gtmla01.x400.gc.ca

Republic of Guinea
Canadian Embassy: PO Box 99, **Conakry**, (011-244) 41-23-95; Fax: (011-224) 41-42-36; Email: MITNET: 311-3000; Telex: 2170 (2170 DOMCAN GE); Ambassador, Denis Briand; Counsellor & Consul, Development, J.-C. Mailhot

Republic of Guinea-Bissau *c/o* Republic of Senegal

Co-operative Republic of Guyana
Canadian High Commission: High & Young Sts., **Georgetown**, (011-592-2) 72081; Fax: (011-592-2) 58380; Email: MITNET: 398-0000; Cable: DOMCAN GEORGETOWN; Postal Address: PO Box 10880, Georgetown, Guyana; High Commissioner, Alan Bowker; First Secretary, Development, S. Greaves; First Secretary, Development, D.J. Ross

Republic of Haiti
Canadian Embassy: Édifice Banque de Nova Scotia; rte de Delmas, **Port-au-Prince**, (011-509) 21-2158; Fax: (011-509) 21-8720; Email: MITNET: 310-0000; Telex: (203) 20069 (20069 DOMCAN HN); Cable: DOMCAN PORT-AU-PRINCE; Postal Address: CP 826, Port-au-Prince, Haiti; Ambassador, J. Christopher Poole; Counsellor & Consul, L.-R. Daigle; Counsellor, Development, M. Apollon; Counsellor, Development, S. Fortin

Holy See

Via della Conciliazione 4/D, 00193, Rome

(011-39-6)6830-7316 or fax: (011-39-6)6880-6283

Email: MITNET: 464-0000

Republic of Honduras

Canadian Embassy: Edificio Commercial Los Castatnos; 60 piso, Blvd. **Morazán**, Tegucigalpa, (011-504) 31-45-35; Fax: (011-504) 31-57-93; Telex: 1683 (DOMCA H0); Postal Address: Apartado Postal 3552, Tegucigalpa, Honduras; Ambassador (located in San José, Costa Rica), Dan Goodleaf; Counsellor & Consul (located in Costa Rica), G. Lapointe; Counsellor, Development (located in Costa Rica), J. Touzel

Hong Kong

Commission for Canada: Tower 1, Exchange Square: 8 Connaught Place, 11th Fl., **Hong Kong**, (011-852) 2810-4321; Fax: (011-852) 2810-6736; Email: td.hkong@hkong02.x400.gc.ca; Cable: DOMCAN HONG KONG; Postal Address: GPO Box 11142, Hong Kong, Hong Kong; Commissioner, Garrett C.M. Lambert; Counsellor, Commercial, S. Mullin; First Secretary (Commercial), Martin Charron, Email: martin.charron@hkong.02.400.gc.ca; Commercial Officer, Zita Yau

Republic of Hungary

Canadian Embassy: Budakeszi ut. 32, 1121, Budapest, (011-36-1) 275-1200; Fax: (011-36-1) 275-1210; Email: MITNET: 393-0000; Ambassador, Susan

M.W. Cartwright; Counsellor, S. Marcoux; Counsellor & Consul, Commercial, R. Lecoq; Commercial Officer, Ilona Csete-Horvath, Email: ilona.csete-horvath@bpestanx01.400.gc.ca

Republic of Iceland *c/o* Kingdom of Norway
Reykjavik: Hon. Consul General, J.H. Bergs, Honorary Consulate General of Canada, Suourlandsbraut 10, 108, Reykjavik, Iceland, (011-354-5) 680-820; Fax: (011-354-5) 680-899: Telex: 94014879 (CAND G); Postal Address: PO Box 8094, 128 Reykjavik, Iceland

Republic of India
Canadian High Commission: 7/8 Shantipath, **Chanakyapuri**, New Delhi 110021, (011-91-11) 687-6500; Fax: (011-91-11) 687-6579; Email: MITNET: 355-0000; Cable: DOMCANADA NEW DELHI; Postal Address: PO Box 5207, New Delhi, India; High Commissioner, Stanley Gooch; Deputy High Commissioner, D. Waterfall; Counsellor, Commercial, D. Summers; Counsellor, Development, S. Gibbons; Commercial Officer, Viney Gupta, Email: viney.gupta@delhi01.x400.gc.ca; Bangalore: Canadian Trade Office, 103 Prestige Meridien 1, 29 M.G. Rd., Bangalore, India, (011-92-80) 559-9418; Fax: (011-91-80) 559-9424; Bombay: Consul & Trade Commissioner, D.C. Dix, Canadian Consulate, 41/43 Maker Chambers VI, 6 Jamnalal Bajaj Marg, Nariman Point, **Bombay**, 400 021, India, . (011-91-22) 287-6027; Fax: (011-91-22) 287-5514; Telex: 011-85122 (CIC IN); Madras: Hon. Consul, V. Srinivasan, Honorary Consulate of Canada, c/o W.S. Industries Limited,

Karumuttu Centre, 498 Anna Salai, 2nd Fl., Nandanam, Madras 600 035, India, 434-9295; Fax: 434-0847

Republic of Indonesia

Canadian Embassy: Wisma Metropolitan, Jalan Jendral Sudirman, 5th Fl., **Jakarta** 12084, (011-62-21) 525-0709; Fax: (011-62-21) 571-2251; Email: MITNET: 344-0000; Postal Address: PO Box 8324/JKS.MP, Jakatarta 12084, Indonesia; Ambassador, Gary Smith; Counsellor & Consul, A. McNiven; Counsellor, Development, R. Woodhouse; Counsellor & Consul, Commercial, G. Rishchynski; Commercial Officer, Husni Djaelani, Email: djaelani.husni@jkrta02.x400.gc.ca; Surabaya: A. Markus, Hon. Consul, Honorary Consulate of Canada, c/o P.T. Maspion, Head Office, JL, Kembang Jepun, No. 38-40, Surabaya, Indonesia, 031-330333; Fax: 031-333055

Islamic Republic of Iran

Canadian Embassy: 57 Shahid Sarafraz, Ostad-Motahari Ave., 15868, **Tehran**, (011-98-21) 873-2623; Fax: (011-98-21) 873-3202; Email: MITNET: 330-3920; Postal Address: PO Box 11365-4647, Tehran, Iran; Ambassador, Michel de Salaberry; Counsellor & Consul, G. Jacoby; Counsellor, Commercial, G. Rarrman; Third Secretary (Commercial), Emmanuel Kamarianakis, Email: emmanuel.kamarianakis@teran01.x400.gc.ca

Republic of Iraq *c/o* Hashemite Kingdom of Jordan

Republic of Ireland

Canadian Embassy: 65 St. Stephen's Green, **Dublin** 2, (011-353-1) 478-1988; Fax: (011-353-1) 478-1285; Email: MITNET: 441-0000; Cable: DOMCAN DUBLIN; Ambassador, Michael B. Phillips; Counsellor, Commercial, K. Dewolf; Commercial Officer, John Sullivan

State of Israel

Canadian Embassy: 220 Rehov Hayarkon, **Tel Aviv** 63405, (011-972-3) 527-2929; Fax: (011-972-3) 527-2333; Email: MITNET: 399-0000; Postal Address: PO Box 6410, Tel Aviv 63405, Israel; Ambassador, David Berger; Counsellor & Consul, D. Viveash; High Commissioner, Cyprus, David Berger; Counsellor, Commercial, R. Zeisler; Canadian Forces Attaché, Col. T.S.M. Humphries; Commercial Officer, Atalia Kahan, Email: atalia.kahan@taviv.01.x400.gc.ca

Italian Republic

Canadian Embassy: Via G.B. de Rossi 27, 00161, **Rome**, (011-39-6) 44598-1; Fax: (011-39-6) 44598-750; Email: rome@rome01.x400.gc.ca: MITNET: 455-0000; Cable: DOMCAN ROME; Ambassador, Jeremy Kinsman; Minister-Counsellor, R.F. Andrigo; Minister-Counsellor, Economic/Commercial, N. Kalisch; Counsellor, Development, G. Saint Cyr; Commercial Officer, Alex L. Jones, Email: alex.jones@rome01.x400.gc.ca; **Milan**: Consul General, Ian McLean, Canadian Consulate General, Via Vittor Pisani 19, 20124, Milan, Italy, (011-39-2) 6758-1; Fax: (011-39-2) 6758-3900; URL: http://www.Agora.stm.it/canaca/homepage.htm: Email: milan@milan01.x400.gc.ca

Republic of the Ivory Coast

Canadian Embassy: Immeuble Trade Centre: 23, av Noguès, Le Plateau, **Abidjan**, (011-225) 21-20-09; Fax: (011-225) 22-95-30; Email: MITNET: 325-0000: Telex: 23593 (DOMCAN CI); Cable: DOMCAN CI; Postal Address: PO Box 4104, Abidjan 01, Côte d'Ivoire; Ambassador, Suzanne Laporte; Counsellor & Consul, G. Paquet; First Secretary, Commercial, P. Veilleux; Commercial Officer, Ousmane Somali

Jamaica

Canadian High Commission: Mutual Security Bank Bldg., 30-36 Knutsford Blvd., **Kingston** 5, 809/926-1500; Fax: 809/926-1702; Email: MITNET: 333-0000; Telex: 2130 (2130 BEAVER JA); Cable; BEAVER KINGSTONJA; Postal Address: PO Box 1500, Kingston 10, Jamaica; High Commissioner, Gavin Stewart; Counsellor, Commercial, P. Molson; Montego Bay: Hon. Consul, L. Crichton, Consulate of Canada, 29 Gloucester Ave., Montego Bay, Jamaica, 809/952-6198; Fax: 809/952-3953

Japan

Canadian Embassy: 3-38 Akasaka 7-chome, Minatoku, **Tokyo** 107, (011-81-3) 3408-2101; Fax: (011-81-3) 3479-5320; Telex: (72) 22218 (DOMCAN J22218); Cable: CANADIAN TOKYO; Trade & Investment Section, (011-81-3) 3470-7280; Ambassador, Donald W. Campbell; Minister, Economic/Commercial, J. Tennant; Counsellor, Commercial, R. Brocklebank; Commercial Officer, Yoshio Tamai, Email: yoshio.tamai@tokyo04.x400.gc.ca; Fukuoka: Consul & Trade Commissioner, B. Préfontaine, Consulate of

Canada, FT Bldg., 9F, 4-8-28 Watanabe-Dori, Chuo-Ku, Fukuoka, Japan 810, (011-81-92) 752-6055; Fax: (011-81-92) 752-6077; Nagoya: Consul & Trade Commissioner, Robert Mason, Consulate of Canada, Nakato Marunouchi Bldg., 6F, 3-7-16 Marunouchi, Naka-Ku, Nagoya, Japan, (011-81-52) 972-0450; Fax: (011-81-52) 972-0453; Osaka 542: Consul General, Peter Campbell, Consulate General of Canada, Daisan Shoho Bldg., 12th Fl., 2-2-3, Nishi-Shinsaibashi, Chuo-ku, Osaka 542, Japan, (011-81-6) 212-4910; Fax: (011-81-6) 212-4914; Postal Address: PO Box 150, Osaka Minami 542-91, Japan

Hashemite Kingdom of Jordan
Canadian Embassy: Pearl of Shmeisani Bldg., Amman, (011-962-6) 66-61-24; Fax: (011-962-6) 68-92-27; Email: MITNET: 391-0000; Postal Address: PO Box 815403, Amman 11180, Jordan; Ambassador, Michel de Salaberry; Counsellor & Consul, Political, P.A. Bakewell; First Secretary, Development, D. Joly; Commercial Officer, Hala Helou

Republic of Kazakhstan
Canadian Embassy: 34 Vinagradova St., Almaty, (011-7-327) 250-11-51; Fax: (011-7-327) 581-14-93; Ambassador, Richard Mann; Minister-Counsellor, Commercial (located in Russia), M.L. Morin; Counsellor, Commercial (located in Russia), G. Jones

Republic of Kenya
Canadian High Commission: Comcraft House: Hailé Sélassie Ave., Nairobi,

(011-254-2) 21-48-04; Fax: (011-254-2) 22-69-87; Email: MITNET: 331-3400; Telex: 22198 (22198 DOMCAN); Cable: DOMCAN NAIROBI; Postal Address: PO Box 30481, **Nairobi**, Kenya; High Commissioner, Bernard Dussault; Counsellor, J. Wall; Counsellor, Development, J. Lobsinger; Senior Commercial Assistant, Thelma R. Staussi

Kiribati *c/o* New Zealand

Republic of Korea
Canadian Embassy: 10th Fl., Kolon Bldg., 45 Mugyo-Dong, 10th/11th Fls., Jung-Ku, **Seoul** 100-170, (011-82-2) 753-2605; Fax: (011-82-2) 755-0686; Email: MITNET: 348-0000; Cable: DOMCAN SEOUL; Postal Address: PO Box 6299, Seoul 100-662, Korea; Ambassador, Michel Perrault; Minister, Counsellor & Consul, Commercial, M. Hladik; Counsellor, Commercial, M. Woods; Third Secretary, Commercial, Jean-Dominique Ieraci, Email: jean-dominique.j.d.i.ieraci@seoul02.x400.gc.ca; Commercial Officer, Y.H. Choi; Pusan: Hon. Consul, H.-W. Koo, Honorary Consulate of Canada, c/o Bumin Mutual Savings & Finance Corporation, #32-1, 2-GA, Daecheung-Dong, Chung-Ku, Pusan, Korea, (011-8251) 246-7024; Fax: (011-8251) 247-8443

State of Kuwait
Canadian Embassy: Block 4, House No. 24: Al-Mutawakel, Da Aiyah, **Kuwait City**, (011-965) 256-3025; Fax: (011-965) 256-4167; Email: MITNET: 322-0000; Postal Address: PO Box 25281, Safat 13113, Kuwait City, Kuwait; Ambassador, Terry Colfer; Counsellor & Consul, Commercial,

J.N. Guérin; Counsellor & Consul, Commercial, R. Banerjee; Commercial Officer, Ibtissam Hajj

Republic of Kyrgyzstan *c/o* Republic of Kazakhstan

Lao People's Democratic Republic *c/o* Kingdom of Thailand

Republic of Latvia
Canadian Embassy: Doma laukums 4, 4th Fl., Riga, (011-371) 783-0141; Fax: (011-371) 783-0140; Ambassador (located in Sweden), William L. Clarke; First Secretary, Commercial, H.J. Kunzer

Lebanese Republic
Office of the Canadian Embassy: Coolrite Bldg., 1st Fl., 434 Autostrade Jall-El-Dib, **Beirut**, (011-961-1) 521-163; Fax: (011-961-1) 521-167; Postal Address: PO Box 60163, Jal-El-Dib, Beirut, Lebanon; Ambassador, Daniel Marchand; Second Secretary & Vice Counsel, Commercial, M. Poirier; Counsellor, Commercial, M. Abou Guendia; Second Secretary, Commercial, Mario Poirier

Kingdom of Lesotho *c/o* South Africa
Maseru: Hon. Consul, Z.M. Bam, Honorary Consulate of Canada, Canadian Consulate, Maseru Book Centre Kingsway, 1st Fl., PO Box 1165, Maseru, Lesotho, (011-266) 311-256; Fax: (011-266) 310-462

Republic of Liberia *c/o* Republic of Ghana

Social People's Libyan Arab Jamahiriya *c/o* Republic of Tunisia

Pricipality of Liechtenstein *c/o* Swiss Confederation

Republic of Lithuania
Canadian Embassy: Didzioji 8-5, 2001, Vilnius, (011-370-2) 220-898; Fax: (011-370-2) 220-884; Ambassador (located in Sweden), William L. Clarke; Minister-Counsellor (located in Latvia), G.R. Skinner; First Secretary, Commercial (located in Latvia), J.H. Kunzer

Grand Duchy of Luxembourg *c/o* Kingdom of Belgium
Luxembourg: Hon. Consul, P. Krier, Honorary Consulate of Canada, c/o Price-Waterhouse & Co., 24-26, av de la Liberté, Luxembourg L-1930, Luxembourg, (011-352) 40-24-20; Fax: (011-352) 40-24-55 ext. 600

Macao *c/o* Hong Kong

Democratic Republic of Madagascar *c/o* United Republic of Tanzania
Antananarivo 101: Hon. Consul, Serge P. Lachapelle, Honorary Consulate of Canada, c/o QIT-Madagascar Minerals, Villa Paula Androhibe, Lot II-J-169, Antananarivo 101, Madagascar, (011-261-2) 425-59; Fax: (011-251-2) 425-06; Telex: 22474 BAWDEN MG; Postal Address: Canadian Consulate, CP 4003, Antananarivo 101, Madagascar

Madeira *c/o* Portuguese Republic

Republic of Malawi *c/o* Republic of Zambia
Blantyre-Limbe: Hon. Consul, K. Okhai, Honorary Consulate of Canada, Comet Ltd., PO Box 51146, Blantyre-Limbe, Malawi, (011-265) 643-277; Fax: (011-265) 643-446

Malaysia
Canadian High Commission: Plaza MBF: 172 Jalan Ampang, 7th Fl., 50450, **Kuala Lumpur**, (011-60-3) 261-2000; Fax: (011-60-3) 261-3248; Email: tradcan@po.jaring.my; MITNET: 345-0000; Postal Address: PO Box 10990, 50732, Kuala Lumpur, Malaysia; High Commissioner, André Simard; Counsellor, Commercial, P.S. Lau; Counsellor, Commercial, B. Reid; First Secretary, ?Commercial, Paul Bailey

Republic of Maldives *c/o* Democratic Socialist Republic of Sri Lanka

Republic of Mali
Canadian Embassy: PO Box 198, Bamako, (011-223) 22-22-36; Fax: (001-223) 22-43-62; Telex: 2530 (DOMCAN BAMAKO); Ambassador, Susan McCoy; Counsellor & Consul, Development, Denis G. Beaudoin

Republic of Malta *c/o* Italian Republic
Valletta: Hon. Consul, J.M. Demajo, Honorary Consulate of Canada, Demajo

---

House, 103 Archbishop St., Valletta, Malta, (011-356) 233-121; Fax: (011-356) 235-145

Marshall Islands *c/o* Republic of the Philippines

Martinique *c/o* Barbados

Islamic Republic of Mauritania *c/o* Republic of Senegal
Nouakchott: Hon. Consul, J. Chauvin, Honorary Consulate of Canada, PO Box 428, Nouakchott, Mauritania, (011-222-2) 534-48; Fax: (011-222-2) 540-09

Republic of Mauritius *c/o* Republic of South Africa
Port Louis: Hon. Consul, M.P. Birger, Canadian Consulate, 18 Jules Koenij St., Port Louis, Mauritius, (011-230) 208-0821; Fax: (011-230) 208-3391

United Mexican States
Canadian Embassy: Calle Schiller no.529, Colonia Pollanco, 11560, **Mexico City**, (011-52-5) 724-7900; Fax: (011-52-5) 724-7981; Email: MITNET: 379-3000; Postal Address: Apartado Postal 105-05, 11580 Mexico City, D.F. Mexico; Ambassador, Marc Perron; Minister-Counsellor, Economic/Commercial, D. Thibault; Counsellor, Commercial, J. Prévost; Counsellor, Commercial, M. Wondergem; Counsellor, Commerce, B. Hood; Second Secretary, Commercial, Sophie Legendre; Acapulco: Hon. Consul, Diane McLean,

Honorary Consulate of Canada, Hotel club del Sol, Costera Miguel Aleman, esq. Reyes Católicos, Acapulco, Mexico, (011-52-74) 85-66-21; Fax: (011-52-74) 85-74-17; Postal Address: Apartado Postal 94-C, 39300, **Acapulco**, Guerrero, Mexico; Ajijic: Hon. Consul, A.C. Rose, Honorary Consulate of Canada, Hotel de Chapala, Paseo del Prado 20, Ajijic, Mexico, (011-52-376) 62-288; Fax: (011-52-376) 62-420; Cancun: Hon. Consul, Daniel Lavoie, Honorary Consulate of Canada, Centro Commercial Plaza Mexico, Local 312, Ava. Tulum 200, esq. Agua, 77500, **Cancun**, Mexico, (011-52-98) 84-37-16; Fax: (011-52-98) 84-67-16; Guadalajara: Consul & Trade Commissioner, J. Daubeny, Canadian Consulate, Hotel Fiesta Americana, Local 31, Aurelio Aceves 225, Col. Vallarta Poniente, 44100, Guadalajara, Mexico, (011-52-36) 16-56-42; Fax: (011-52-36) 15-86-65; **Mazatlan**: Hon. Consul, F. Balcarcel, Honorary Consulate of Canada, Hotel Playa Mazatlan, Zona Dorada, Rodolfo Loaiza 202, Mazatlan, Mexico, (011-52-69) 13-73-20; Fax: (011-52-69) 14-66-55; Postal Address: Apartado Postal 614, 82210, Mazatlan, Sinaloa, Mexico; Monterrey: Vice-Consul & Trade Commissioner, T.G. Cullen, Canadian Consulate, Edificio Kalos, Pisco C-1, Local 108-A, Zaragoza 1300 Sury Constitucion, 6400, **Monterrey**, Mexico, (011-52-83) 44-27-53; Fax: (011-52-83) 44-30-48; Oaxaca: Hon. Consul, Frances May, Honorary Consulate of Canad, 119 Dr. Liceaga #8,68000, **Oaxaco**, Mexico, (011-52-95) 13-37-77; Fax: (011-52-95) 15-21-47; Postal Address: Apartado Postal 29 Sucursal C, Col. Reforma, 68050 Oaxaco, Mexico; Puerto Vallarta: Hon. Consul, L. Benoit, Honorary Consulate of Canada, Calle Hidalgo 226, 160 Zaragoza,

Interior 10, Col, Centro, 48300, Puerto Vallarta, Mexico, (011-52-32) 22-53-98; Fax: (011-52-32) 22-35-17; San Miguel de Allende: Hon. Consul, G. Bisaillon, Honorary Consulate of Canada, Mesones 38, Interior 15, 37700, San Miguel de Allende, Mexico, (011-52-41) 52-30-25; Fax: (011-52-41) 52-68-56; **Tijuana**: Hon. Consul, R.E. Ripa, Honorary Consulate Canada, German Gedovius 10411-101, Condominio del Parque, Zona Rio, 22320, Tijuana, Mexico, (011-52-66) 84-04-61; Fax: (011-52-66) 84-03-01

Republic of Moldova *c/o* Republic of Romania

Principality of Monaco *c/o* French Republic

Mongolian People's Republic *c/o* People's Republic of China

Montenegro *c/o* Federal Republic of Yugoslavia

Republic of Mozambique
Embassy of Mozambique (to Canada): #570, 1990 M St. NW, **Washington** DC 20036, 202/293-7146; Fax: 202/835-0245; Ambassador, His Exellency Hipolito Pereira Zozimo Patricio

Union of Myanmar
Embassy of Myanmar #902, 85 Range Rd., **Ottawa** ON K1N 8J6, 613/232-6434; Fax: 613/232-6435; Ambassador, His Excellency Dr. Kyaw Winung

Republic of Namibia

High Commission for Namibia (to Canada): 1605 New Hampshire Ave. NW, **Washington** DC 20009, 202/986-0540; Fax: 202/986-0443; High Commissioner, His Excellency Tuliameni Kalomoh; **Waterloo**: Hon. Consul, Walter McLean, 122 Avondale Ave. South, Waterloo ON N2L 2G3, 51978-5932; Fax: 519/578-7799

Kingdom of Nepal

Royal Nepalese Embassy (to Canada): c/o Embassy of Nepal, 2131 Leroy Place NW, **Washington** DC 20008, 202/667-4550; Fax: 202/667-5534; Telex 440085 EVER UI; Ambassador, Vacant; Chargé d'Affaires, Pradep Khapitwada; **Toronto**: Hon. Consul General, Kunjar Sharma, BDO Dunwoody Ward Mallette, Royal Bank Plaza, PO Box 33, Toronto ON M5J 2J9, 416/865-0210; Fax: 416/865-0904

Kingdom of the Netherlands

Royal Netherlands Embassy: #2020, 350 Albert St., **Ottawa** ON K1R 1A4, 613237-5030; Fax: 613/237-6471; Ambassador, His Excellency Johannes H.W. Fietelaars; Counsellor & Deputy Head of Mission, Arend H. Huitzing; Counsellor, Economic & Commercial Affairs, Aart Jan M. Verdegaal; **Calgary**: Hon. Consul, G.A. Van Wielingen, Canada Trust Tower, #2103, 421 - 7 Ave. SW, Calgary AB T2P 4K9, 403/266-2710; Fax: 403/265-8180; **Edmonton**: Hon. Consul, R. Dootjes, 10214 - 112 St., Edmonton AB T5K 1M5, 403428-7513; Fax: 403/424-2053; Halifax: Hon. Consul, Gavin Joseph

Rainnie, Purdy's Wharf, #1306, 1959 Upper Water St., **Halifax** NS B3J 3N2, 902/422-1485; Fax: 902/420-1787; **Kingston**: Hon. Vice Consul, Dr. H. Westenberg, 115 Lower Union St., Kingston ON K7L 2N3, 613/542-7095; **London**: Hon. Vice Consul, Dr. R.D. ter-Vrugt, 650 Colborne St., London ON N5A 5A1, 519/551-0453; Fax: 519/432-7431; Montréal: Consul General, Hans van Dam, #1500, 1245, rue Sherbrooke ouest, **Montréal** PQ H3G 1G2, 514/849-4347; Fax: 514/849-8260; Québec: Hon. Consul, E.A. Price, 10, rue Ate-Anne, PO Box 833, Québec PQ G1R 3X1, 418/692-2175; Fax: 418/692-4161; **Regina**: Hon. Consul, W.B.C. de Lint, #100, 2400 College Ave., Regina SK S4P 1C8, 306/522-8577; Saint John: Hon. Consul, C.D. Whelly, #1600, 1 Brunswick Sq., PO Box 1324, Stn A, Saint John NB E2L 4H8, 506/632-8900; Fax: 506/632-8809; Telex: 014-47252; **St. John's**: Hon. Consul, A.A. Bruneau, 55 Kenmount Rd., PO Box 8910, St. John's NF A1B 3P6, 709737-5616; Fax: 709/737-5832; Thunder Bay: Hon. Vice Consul, R.P. Welter, 179 South Algoma St., Thunder Bay ON P7B 3C1, 807/344-5721; **Toronto**: Consul General, P.W.A. Schellekeus, #2106, 1 Dudnas St., West, Toronto ON M5G 1Z3, 416/598-2520; Fax: 416/589-8064; **Vancouver**: Consul General, Baron M. Van Aerssen Beijeren Van Voshol, Crown Trust Bldg., #821, 475 Howe St., Vancouver BC V6C 2B3, 604/684-6448; Fax: 604/684-3549; **Winnipeg:** Hon. Consul, Hans Hasenack, 69 Shorecrest Dr., Winnipeg MB R3P 1N9, 204/489-0467; Fax: 204-489-4219

Netherlands Antilles

Maduro and Curiels Bank N.V., Plaza JoJo Correa 2-4, Willemstad, Curacao; (011-599-9)66-11-15 or fax: (01-599-9)66-11-22

New Caledonia c/o Commonwealth of Australia

New Zealand

61 Molesworth St., 3rd Floor, Thorndon, **Wellington**; P.O.Box 12-049, Thorndon, Wellington, New Zealand; (011-64-4)473-9577 or fax: (011-64-4)471-2082 or cable: DOMCAN WELLINGTON; Email: MITNET:352-0000; Jetset Centre, Level 9, 44-48 Emily Place, Auckland, New Zealand; P.O. Box 6186, Wellesley St., Auckland, New Zealand; (011-64-9)309-3690 or fax: (011-64-9)307-3111

Republic of Nicaragua

Frente Plazoleta Telcor Central, 208 Calle de Triunfo, **Managua**, Nicaragua; Apartado 514, Managua, Nicaragua
(011-505-2)28-75-74 or fax: (011-505-2)28-48-21

Republic of Niger

Edifice Sonara II.: av du Premier Pont, Niamey; CP 362, Niamey, Niger
(011-227)73-36-86 or fax: (011-227)55-31-01;
Telex: 5264 (DOMCAN 5264 NI)

Federal Republic of Nigeria

Committee of Vice-Chancellors Bldg., Plot 8A, 4 Idowa-Taylor St., Victoria Island, **Lagos**; P.O. Box 54506, Ikoyi Station, Lagos, Nigeria
(011-234-1)262-2512 or fax: (011-234-1)262-2517 or cable DOMCAN LAGOS

Telex: 21275 (DOMCAN NG); Liaison Office, Plot 622, Gana St., Zone A5, Maitama, Abuja, Nigeria; P.O. Box 6924 WUSE, Abuja FCT, Nigeria (011)-234-090)803-249 or fax: (011-234-090)803-249

Niue c/o New Zealand

Northern Ireland c/o United Kingdom of Great Britain & Northern Ireland

Northern Marianas c/o Republic of the Philippines

Kingdom of Norway
Oscars Gate 20, Oslo 0244; (011-47)22-46-69-55 or fax: (011-47)22-69-34-67
Email: td.oslo@oslo 0.1x400.gc.ca

Sultanate of Oman
Flat #310, Bldg. 477, Moosa Abdul Rahman Hassan Bldg., Way 2907, A'Noor St., Ruwi, Muscat, Oman; P.O. Box 8275, Muttrah, Sultanate of Oman; (011-968)791-738 or fax: (011-968)791-740

Islamic Republic of Pakistan
Diplomatic Enclave: Sector G-5, Islamabad; P.O. Box 1042, Islamabad, Pakistan; (011-92-51)21-111-01 or fax: (011-92-51)21-15-40 or cable: DOMCAN ISLAMABAD; #120, Beach Luxury Hotel, Moulvi Tamiz, Uddin Khan Rd., Karachi 0227, Pakistan; (011-92-21)55-11-00 or fax: (011-92-21)55-12-22

Republic of Panama

Edifico Banco Central Hispano: Ave. Samuel Lewis 4th Floor, **Panama City**, Apartado 3658, Balboa Ancon, Panama City, Panama; (011-507)264-9731 or fax: (011-507)264-0451; Edifico Proconsa, Aero Peru, Piso 5B, Calle Manuel y Caza, Campo Alegre, Panama City, Panama; Apartado Postal 3658, Balboa, Panama; (011-507)64-70-14 or fax: (011-507)23-54-70

Papua New Guinea

The Lodge, Brampton St., 2nd Fl., Port Moresby, Papua New Guinea; P.O. Box 851, Port Moresby, **Papua** New Guinea; (011-675)21-35-99 or fax: (011-675)21-36-12

Republic of Paraguay

El Paraguayo Independiente 995, Entrepiso, Officinas 1 y 2, **Asuncion**, Paraguay; Cassilla 2577, Asuncion, Paraguay; (011-595-21)49-95-05 or fax: (011-595-21)44-95-06; Telex: 652-PY (652-PY COTMO)

Republic of Peru

Calle Federico Gerdes 130 (antes Libertad); Miraflores, **Lima**; Casilla 18-1126, Correo Miraflores, Lima 18, Peru; (011-51-1)444-4015 or fax: (011-51-1)444-4347 or cable: CANADIAN LIMA; Telex: 25323 PE DOMCANP)
Commercial Officer Email: oscar.vasquez@lima0.1x400.gc.ca

Republic of the Philippines

Allied Bank Centre, 9th & 11th Floors, 6754 Ayala Ave., **Makati City**, Manila (postal address) P.O.Box 2168, Makati

Central Post Office, 1299 Makati, **Manila Metro**, Philippines

(011-63-2)810-8861 or fax: (011-63-2)810-8839 or cable DOMCAN MANILA

Telex:63676 (63676 DOMCAN PN)

Commercial Officer Email: byron.lee@manil01.x400.gc.ca

Republic of Poland

Ulica Jana Matejki 1/5, **Warsaw** 00-481

(011-48-22)629-80-51 or fax: (011-48-22)629-64-57

Email: wsaw.td@wsa01.x400.gc.ca

Portuguese Republic

Ava. da Liberdade 144/56, 4th Floor, **Lisbon** 1250

(011-351-1)347-4892 or fax: (011-351-1)347-6466 or cable

DOMCAN LISBON

Commercial Officer Email: luis.damaso@lsbon01.x400.gc.ca

Rua Frei Lourenco de Sta Maria No. 1, 1st Floor, Apt. 79, Faro 8001, Portugal

(011-351-89)80-37-57 or fax: (011-7-812)119-8448 or fax (011-7-812)119-8393

Rwandese Republic

Rue Akagera, P.O. Box 1177, Kigali

(011-250)73210 or fax: (011-250)72719

Telex: 22592 (22592 DOMCAN RW)

Saint Kitts and Nevis c/o Barbados

Saint Lucia c/o Barbados

Republic of San Marino c/o Italian Republic

Democratic Republic of Sao Tome & Principe c/o Gabonese Republic

Kingdom of Saudi Arabia
Diplomatic Quarter: Riyadh; P.O. Box 94321, Riyadh 11693, **Saudi Arabia**
(011-966-1)488-2288 or fax: (011-966-1)488-1997 or cable: DOMCAN RIYADH
Telex: 404893 (DOMCAN SJ); Commercial Officer Email:
david.d.m.mcgregor@ryadh01.x400.gc.ca
Headquarters Bldg., Zahid Corporate Group, Jeddah, Saudi Arabia
P.O. Box 8929, Jeddah 2149, Saudi Arabia

Scotland c/o United Kingdom of Great Britain & Northern Ireland

Republic of Senegal
45, av de la Republique, **Dakar**; CP 3373, Dakar, Senegal
(011-221)23-92-90 or fax: (011-221)23-87-49

Serbia c/o Federal Republic of Yugoslavia

Republic of Seychelles c/o United Republic of Tanzania

Republic of Sierra Leone c/o Republic of Ghana

Republic of Singapore

IBM Towers: 80 Anson Road, 14th/15th Floors, Singapore 0207; Robinson Road, P.O. Box 845 **Singapore** 9016, Singapore; (011-65)225-6363 or fax: (011-65)225-2450 or cable: CANADIAN SINGAPORE; Email: cdatanjs@signet.com.sg

Slovak Republic

Kolarska 4, 81106, Bratislava, Slovakia; (011-42-07)361-277

Republic of Slovenia c/o Republic of Hungary

Solomon Islands c/o Commonwealth of Australia

Somali Democratic Republic c/o Republic of Kenya

Republic of South Africa

1103 Arcadia St., Hatfield 0083, **Pretoria** (011-221)23-87-49
(011-322)301197 or fax: (011-322)031024
Canadian High Commission Trade Office, Cradock Place, 10 Arnol St., 1st Floor, Rosebank, **Johannesburg**, South Africa (postal address) Canadian High Commission Trade Office, P.O. Box 1394, Parkland
2121, Johannesburg, South Africa

Kingdom of Spain
Edificio Goya: Calle Nunez de Balboa 35, **Madrid** 28001
(postal address) Apartado 587, 28080 Madrid, Spain
(011-34-1)431-4300 or fax: (011-34-1)431-3893 or cable
CANADIAN MADRID; Commercial Officer Email:
isidro.garcia@mdrid01.x400.gc.ca
Travessera de les Corts, 265 **Barcelona** 08014, Spain
(011-34-3)410-6699 or fax: (011-34-3)410-7755
Ava. Juan Antonia Zunzunegui, 2, 1, Bilbao 4813, Spain
(011-34-4)427-69-22) or fax: (011-34-4)427-15-78
Plaza de la Malagueta 3, 1st Floor, Malaga 29016, Spain
(011-34-52)22-33-46 or fax: (011-34-52)22-40-23
Ava. de la Constitucion 30, 2nd Floor, local 4-41001, **Seville**, Spain
(011-34-54)22-94-13

Republic of Sri Lanka
6 Gregory's Rd., Cinnamon Gardens, **Colombo** 7
(postal address) P.O. Box 1006, Colombo, Sri Lanka
(011-94-1)69-58-41 or fax: (011-94-1)68-70-49 or cable
DOMCANADA COLOMBO

St. Martin/St-Marten c/o Barbados

Republic of The Sudan c/o Democratic Republic of Ethiopia

Republic of Suriname

Waterkant 90-94, P.O. Box 1849-1850, **Paramaribo**, Suriname

(011-597)471-222 or fax: (011-597)475-718

Kingdom of Swaziland c/o Republic of South Africa

Kingdom of Sweden

Tegelbacken 4, 7th Fl., Stockholm P.O. Box 16129, 10323; **Stockholm**, Sweden

(011-46-8)453-3000 or fax: (011-46-8)24-24-91

Email: stlkm@stklm01.x400.gc.ca

Commercial Officer Email: inga.olsson@stkhm01.x400.gc.ca

Swiss Confederation

Kirchenfeldstr. 88, Berne 3005 P.O.Box 3000, **Berne** 6, Switzerland

(011-41-31)352-63-81 or fax: (011-41-31)352-73-15

Email: bern.cda@ping.ch

Syrian Arab Republic

Lot 12, Mezzeh Autostr., Damascus

(postal address) P.O. Box 3394 Damascus, Syria

(011-963-11)611-6892 or fax: (011-963-11)611-8034

Republic of Tajikistan c/o Republic of Kazakhstan

United Republic of Tanzania
38 Mirambo St., **Dar-es-Salaam**
(postal address) P.O. Box 1022, Dar-es-Salaam, Tanzania
(011-255-51)46000 or fax: (011-255-51)46005
Telex: 41015 (41015 DOMCAN TZ)

Kingdom of Thailand
Boonmitr Bldg. 138 Silom Rd., 11th Floor, **Bangkok** 10500
P.O. Box 2090, Bangkok 10500, Thailand
(011-66-2)237-4125 or fax: (011-66-2)236-6463
Raming Tea Co. Ltd., 151 Super Hwy, Tasala, Chiang Mai 5000, Thailand
(011-66-53)24-22-92 or fax: (011-66-53)24-26-16

Republic of Togo c/o Republic of Ghana

Kingdom of Tonga c/o New Zealand

Republic of Trinidad & Tobago
Huggins Bldg.: 72 South Quay, Port-of-Spain; P.O. Box 1246,
Port-of-Spain, Trinidad
(809)623-7254 or fax : (809)624-4016Cable: DOMCAN PORT OF SPAIN

Republic of Tunisia
3, rue du Senegal, Place d'Afrique, **Tunis**; P.O. Box 31,
Belvedere, 1002 Tunis, Tunisia

(011-216-1)796-577 or fax: (011-216-1)792-371 or cable DOMCAN TUNIS
Telex: 15324 (15324 DOMCAN TN)

Republic of Turkey
Nenehatun Caddesi No. 75, Gaziosmanpasa 06700, Ankara
(011-90-312)436-1275 or fax: (011-90-312)446-4437
Telex: 42369 (DCAN TR)
Commercial Officer Email: akin.kosetorunu@ankra.01.x400.gc.ca
Buyukdere Cad. 107/3, Begun Han. 80300, Gayrettepe, Istanbul, Turkey
(011-90-1)271-5174 or fax: (011-90-1)272-3427
Telex: 26133 TR

Turkmenistan c/o Republic of Kazakhstan

Turks & Caicos Islands c/o Jamaica

Tuvalu c/o New Zealand

U.S. Virgin Islands c/o United States of America

Republic of Uganda
92/94 - 5 St., Industrial Area, **Kampala**; Uganda Bata, P.O. Box 422,
Kampala, Uganda
(011-256-41))25-81-41 or fax: (011-256-41)24-13-80

Republic of Ukraine
31 Yaroslaviiv Val St., Kiev 252034
(011-7-044)212-0412 or fax: (011-7-044)212-2339
Telex: 131479 (131479 UYUT SU)

United Arab Emirates
Juma Al Majid Bldg., #708, Khalid Ibn Al
Waleed St. Bur **Dubai**, United Arab Emirates
P.O. Box 52472, Dubai, United Arab Emirates
(011-971-4)52-17-17 or fax (011-971-4)51-77-22

United Kingdom of Great Britain & Northern Ireland
Macdonald House: One Grosvenor Sq., London W1X OAB
(011-44-171)258-6600 or fax: (011-44-171)258-6333
Email: MITNET: 445-0000
55 Colmore Row, Birmingham B3 2AS, United Kingdom
(011-44)121-236-6474
3 George St., Edinburgh
(011-32)220-4333

United States of America
501 Pennsylvania Ave. NW, **Washington** DC 20001
(202)682-1740 or fax: (202)682-7726
Telex: 89664 (DOMCAN A WSH)
Email: MITNET: 456-0000;

URL: http://www.nstn.ca/wshdc

Commercial Officer Email: kathryn.aleong@wshdc01.x400.gc.ca

#400 South Tower, One CNN Center, Atlanta, GA 30303-2705

(404)577-6810 or fax: (404)524-5046

Email: MITNET: 467-0000

#400, 3 Copley Place, **Boston** MA 02116

(617)262-3760 or fax: (617)262-3415

Email: MITNET: 468-0000

#3000, 1 Marine Midland Center, **Buffalo** NY 14203-2884

(716)858-9500 or fax: (716)852-4340

Email: MITNET: 469-0000

2 Prudential Plaza, #2400, 180 North Stetson Ave., **Chicago** IL 60601

(312)616-1860 or fax: (312)616-1877

Email: MITNET:470-0000

St. Paul Place, #1700, 750 North St. Paul, **Dallas** TX 75201-3247

(214)922-9806 or fax: (214)922-9815

Cable: CANADIAN DALLAS

Email: MITNET: 472-0000

#1100, 600 Renaissance Center, **Detroit** MI 48243-1798

(313)567-2340 or fax (313)567-2164

URL: http://www.bizserve.com/canadian-detroit

Email: MITNET: 473-0000

550 South Hope St., 9th Floor, **Los Angeles** CA 90071-2627

(213)346-2700 or fax: (213)620-8827

Telex: 674119 (DOMCAN LSA)

#1600, 200 South Biscayne Blvd., **Miami** FL 33131

(305)579-1600 or fax (305)368-3900

Email: MITNET: 368-0000

701 - 4th Ave. South, **Minneapolis** MN 55415

(612)333-4641 or fax: (612)332-4061

Email: MITNET: 474-0000

1251Ave. of the Americas, 16th Floor, **New York** NY 10020-1175

(212)596-1600 or fax: (212)596-1790

URL: http://www.canada-ny.org

Email: MITNET: 457-0000

107 Cereipo St., Alt. de Santa Maria, Guaynabo, **San Juan**, Puerto Rico

(809)790-2210 or fax: (809)790-2205

412 Plaza 600, Sixth & Stewart, **Seattle** WA 98101-1286

(206) 443-1777 or fax: (206)443-1782

Email: MITNET: 477-0000

Eastern Republic of Uruguay

Edifio Torre Libertad: Plaza Cagangha

1335, off. 1105, 11100, Montevideo

(011-598-2)92-20-30) or fax: (011-598-2)92-20-29

Republic of Uzbekistan c/o Republic of Kazakhstan

Republic of Vanuatu c/o Commonwealth of Australia

(011-84-4)235-500 or fax: (011-84-4)235-351

Commercial Officer Email: natalie.n.d.dube@paris03.x400.gc.ca

#102, 203 Dong Khoi St., District 1, **Ho Chi Minh City**, Viet Nam

(011-84-8)242-000 or fax: (011-84-8)294-528

Wales *c/o* United Kingdom of Great Britain & Northern Ireland

Independent State of Western Samoa c/o New Zealand

Republic of Yemen

Yemen Computer Co., Ltd., Bldg 4, Street 11 (near Haddah St.), **Sanaa**, Yemen

 P.O. Box 340, Sanaa, Yemen

(011-967-1)20-88-14 or fax: (011-967-1)20-95-23

Telex: 2406 YCC YE

Federal Republic of Yugoslavia

Kneza Milosa 75, 11000, **Belgrade**

(011-381-11)64-46-66 or fax: (011-381-11)64-14-80 or cable

DOMCAN BELGRADE

Telex: 11137 (11137 DOMCA YU)

Republic of Zaire

c/o Embassy of the USA: 310 av des Aviateurs, Kinshasa

(011-243-12)21-532 or fax (011-243-88)43-805 or cable

AMEMBASSY KINSHASA

Republic of Zambia

5199 United Nation Ave., Lusaka; P.O. Box 31313, **Lusaka**, Zambia;
(011-260-1)25-08-33 or fax: (011-260-1)25-41-76 or cable DOMCAN LUSAKA
Telex: ZA 42480 (DOMCAN ZA 42480)

Republic of Zimbabwe

45 Baines Ave., Harare (postal address) P.O. Box 1430, **Harare**, Zimbabwe;
(011-263-4) 25-08-33 or fax: (011-263-4) 25-41-76 or cable CANAD HARARA
Telex: 24465 (24465 CANADA ZW)

Appendix A: City Codes

The following lists are intended as a guideline and do not contain every city on the aviation map. I have tried to include all of the most popular and most frequented cities. However, it is intended for information purposes only.

North American and International City Codes

	By Code	By City	
	A		

By Code	By City
ABE Allentown Pa.	Aberdeen Scotland ABZ
ABQ Alburquerque N.M.	Acapulco Mexico ACA
ABZ Aberdeen Scotland	Albany New York ALB
ACA Acapulco Mexico	Alburquerque N.M. ABQ
AIY Atlantic City N.J.	Allentown Pa. ABE
AKL Auckland N.Z.	Amsterdam Neth. AMS
ALB Albany New York	Anchorage Alaska ANC
AMS Amsterdam Neth.	Antigua ANU
ANC Anchorage Alaska	Aruba AUA
ANU Antigua	Atlanta Georgia ATL
ATL Atlanta Georgia	Atlantic City N.J. AIY
ATH Athens Greece	Athens Greece ATH
AUA Aruba	Auckland N.Z. AKL
AUS Austin Texas	Austin Texas AUS

B

BCN Barcelona Spain	Baltimore Maryland	BWI
BDA Bermuda	Bangkok Thailand	BKK
BER Berlin Germany	Barbados	BGI
BEY Beirut Lebanon	Barcelona Spain	BCN
BFS Belfast Ireland	Baton Rouge	BTR
BGI Barbados	Beijing China	BJS
BHM Birmingham Alabama	Beirut Lebanon	BEY
BJS Beijing China	Belfast Ireland	BFS
BKK Bangkok Thailand	Berlin Germany	BER
BNA Nashville Tennesse	Bermuda	BDA
BOI Boise Idaho	Birmingham Ala.	BHM
BOM Bombay India	Boise Idaho	BOI
BOS Boston Mass.	Bombay India	BOM
BRU Brussels Belgium	Boston Mass.	BOS
BTR Baton Rouge	Brussels Belgium	BRU
BTV Burlington Vermont	Budapest Hungary	BUD
BUD Budapest Hungary	Bueno Aires	BUE
BUE Bueno Aires	Buffalo New York	BUF
BUF Buffalo New York	Burlington Vermont	BTV
BWI Baltimore Maryland		

C

CAE	Columbia S.C.	Cairo Egypt	CAI
CAI	Cairo Egypt	Cancun Mexico	CUN
CCS	Caracas Venezuela	Caracas Venezuela	CCS
CGN	Cologne Germany	Charleston W.V.	CRW
CHI	Chicago	Charlotte N.C.	CLT
CLE	Cleveland	Chicago	CHI
CLT	Charlotte N.C.	Cincinnati	CVG
CMH	Columbus Ohio	Cleveland	CLE
CPH	Copenhagen Denmark	Cologne Germany	CGN
CRW	Charleston W.V.	Columbia S.C.	CAE
CUN	Cancun Mexico	Columbus Ohio	CMH
CVG	Cincinnati	Copenhagen Denmark	CPH
CZM	Cozumel Mexico	Cozumel Mexico	CZM

E

EDI	Edinburgh Scotland	Edinburgh Scotland
EDIEWR	Newark New Jersey	
EYW	Key West Florida	

F

FLL	Ft. Lauderdale	Fort Myers Fl.	FMY
FMY	Fort Myers Fl.	Frankfurt Germany	FRA
FPO	Freeport Bahamas	Freeport Bahamas	FPO
FRA	Frankfurt Germany	Ft. Lauderdale	FLL

G

GCM	Grand Cayman W.I.	Geneva Switzerland	GVA
GDL	Guadalajara Mexico	Glasgow Scotland	GLA
GEG	Spokane Washington	Grand Caymen W.I.	GCM
GLA	Glasgow Scotland	Grenada	GND
GND	Grenada Windward Is.	Guadalajara Mexico	GDL
GVA	Geneva Switzerland		

H

HAM	Hamburg Germany	Hamburg Germany	HAM
HAR	Harrisburg Pa.	Harrisburg Pa.	HAR
HAV	Havana Cuba	Hartford Ct.	HFD
HEL	Helsinki Finland	Havana Cuba	HAV
HFD	Hartford Ct.	Helsinki Finland	HEL
HKG	Hong Kong	Hong Kong	HKG

HNL	Honolulu	Honolulu	HNL
HOU	Houston Texas	Houston Texas	HOU

I

IND	Indianapolis Indiana	Indianapolis Indiana	IND
IST	Istanbul Turkey	Istanbul Turkey	IST

J

JED	Jeddah Saudi Arabia	Jakarta Indonesia	JKT
JKT	Jakarta Indonesia	Jeddah Saudi Arabia	JED

K

KIN	Kingston Jamaica	Kansas City Mo.	MKC
KUL	Kuala Lumpur Malaysia	Karachi Pakistan	KHI
		Key West Florida	EYW
		Kingston Jamaica	KIN
		Knoxville Tenn.	TYS
		Kuala Lumpur Mal.	KUL

L

LAS	Las Vegas Nevada	Las Vegas Nevada	LAS
LAX	Los Angeles	Lima Peru	LIM
LIM	Lima Peru	Lisbon Portugal	LIS
LIS	Lisbon Portugal	London England	LON
LON	London England	Los Angeles	LAX
		Louisville Kentucky	SDF

M

MAD	Madrid Spain	Madison Wisconsin	MSN
MAN	Manchester England	Madrid Spain	MAD
MBJ	Montego Bay Jamaica	Manchester England	MAN
MEL	Melbourne Australia	Mazatlan Mexico	MZT
MEM	Memphis Tennessee	Melbourne Australia	MEL
MEX	Mexico City Mexico	Memphis Tennessee	MEM
MIA	Miami Florida	Mexico City Mexico	MEX
MIL	Milan Italy	Miami Florida	MIA
MKC	Kansas City Mo.	Milan Italy	MIL
MKE	Milwaukee Wisconsin	Milwaukee Wisconsin	MKE
MNL	Manila Philippines	Minneapolis Minn.	MSP

MOW Moscow Russia

MSN Madison Wisconsin

MSP Minneapolis Minn.

MSY New Orleans

MUC Munich Germany

MZT Mazatlan Mexico

Montego Bay Jamaica	MBJ
Moscow Russia	MOW
Munich Germany	MUC

N

NAS Nassau Bahamas

NCE Nice France

NYC New York N.Y.

Nashville Tennessee	BNA
Nassau Bahamas	NAS
Newark New Jersey	EWR
New Orleans	MSY
New York N.Y.	NYC
Nice France	NCE

O

OAK Oakland California

OMA Omaha Nebraska

ORL Orlando Florida

OSL Oslo Norway

Oakland California	OAK
Omaha Nebraska	OMA
Orlando Florida	ORL
Oslo Norway	OSL

P

PAR	Paris France	Palm Springs	PSP
PBI	West Palm Beach Fl.	Panama City Panama	PTY
PDX	Portland Oregon	Paris France	PAR
PHL	Philadelphia Pa.	Philadelphia Pa.	PHL
PHX	Phoenix Arizona	Phoenix Arizona	PHX
PIT	Pittsburgh Pa.	Pittsburgh Pa.	PIT
POP	Puerto Plata Dom. Rep.	Pointe A Pitre	PTP
POS	Port of Spain	Port of Spain	POS
PRG	Prague Czech.	Portland Maine	PWM
PSP	Palm Springs Ca.	Portland Oregon	PDX
PTP	Pointe A Pitre	Prague Czech.	PRG
PTY	Panama City Panama	Providence R.I.	PVD
PVD	Providence Rhode Is.	Puerto Plata	POP
PVR	Puerto Vallarta Mexico	Puerto Vallarta	PVR
PWM	Portland Maine		

R

RDU	Raleigh N.C.	Raleigh N.C.	RDU
RIO	Rio De Janeiro	Reno Nevada	RNO
RNO	Reno Nevada	Rio De Janeiro	RIO
ROC	Rochester N.Y.	Rochester N.Y.	ROC
ROM	Rome Italy	Rome Italy	ROM

S

SAN	San Diego Ca.	Sacramento Ca.	SMF
SCL	Santiago Chile	Salt Lake City	SLC
SDF	Louisville Kentucky	San Diego Ca.	SAN
SDQ	Santo Domingo	San Francisco	SFO
SEA	Seattle Washington	San Jose Ca.	SJC
SEL	Seoul Korea	San Juan	SJU
SFO	San Francisco	Santiago Chile	SCL
SIN	Singapore	Santo Domingo	SDQ
SJC	San Jose Ca.	Sarasota Florida	SRQ
SJU	San Juan Puerto Rico	Seattle	SEA
SKB	St Kitts Nevis	Seoul Korea	SEL
SLC	Salt Lake City	Singapore	SIN
SLU	St Lucia West Indies	Spokane	GEG
SMF	Sacramento Ca.	St Kitts Nevis	SKB
SRQ	Sarasota Florida	St Louis Missouri	STL
STL	St Louis Missouri	St Lucia	SLU
STO	Stockholm Sweden	St Maarten	SXM
STR	Stuttgart Germany	St Thomas Vir. Is.	STT
STT	St Thomas Virgin Is.	St Vincent W.I.	SVD
SVD	St Vincent W.I.	Stockholm Sweden	STO
SXM	St Maarten	Stuttgart Germany	STR
SYD	Sydney Australia	Sydney Australia	SYD
SYR	Syracuse N.Y.	Syracuse N.Y.	SYR

T

TLV	Tel Aviv Israel	Taipei Taiwan	TPE
TPA	Tampa Florida	Tampa Florida	TPA
TPE	Taipei Taiwan	Tel Aviv Israel	TLV
TUS	Tuscon Arizona	Tokyo Japan	TYO
TYS	Knoxville Tennessee		

V

VCE	Venice Italy	Venice Italy	VCE
VIE	Vienna Austria	Vienna Austria	VIE

W

WAW	Warsaw Poland	Warsaw Poland	WAW
		Washington D.C.	DCA

Z

ZRH	Zurich Switzerland	Zurich Switzerland	ZRH

Note: Bear in mind that these are city codes and not necessarily airport codes. Some airports, like New York, have two airports and although NYC is the city code, your baggage will be checked to the appropriate airport. For example: LGA - Laguardia and JFK - John F. Kennedy

Canadian Cities

YBC Baie Comeau	Bagotville/Saguenay	YBG
YBL Campbell River B.C.	Nanaimo B.C.	YCD
YCG Castlegar B.C.	Deer Lake NFLD.	YDF
YEG Edmonton Alberta	Elliot Lake Ont.	YEL
YHZ Halifax Nova Scotia	Stephenville NFLD.	YJT
YLW Kelowna B.C.	Ottawa Ont.	YOW
YPR Prince Rupert B.C.	Quebec City PQ.	YQB
YQG Windsor Ontario	Yarmouth N.S.	YQI
YQM Moncton New Brunswick	Comox B.C.	YQQ
YQR Regina Saskatchewan	Thunder Bay Ont.	YQT
YQX Gander Newfoundland	Sydney Nova Scotia	YQY
YSB Sudbury Ontario	St John N.B.	YSJ
YSP Marathon Ontario	Timmins Ontario	YTS
YUL Montreal Quebec	Vancouver B.C.	YVR
YWG Winnipeg Manitoba	Cranbrook B.C.	YXC
YXE Saskatoon Saskatchewan	Sioux Lookout Ont.	YXL
YXS Prince George B.C.	London Ontario	YXU
YXX Abbotsford B.C.	North Bay Ontario	YYB
YYC Calgary Alberta	Smithers B.C.	YYD
YYF Penticton B.C.	Charlottetown P.E.I.	YYG
YYJ Victoria B.C.	St Johns NFLD.	YYT
YYZ Toronto Ontario	Yellowknife N.W.T.	YZF

Appendix B: Major Holidays Around the World

Major Canadian Holidays

January 1*
New Year's Day

January 11
Sir John A. MacDonald's Birthday

February 2
Groundhog Day

February 14
Valentine's Day

February 19
Heritage Day and Family Day (Alberta)

March or April*
Good Friday and Easter Monday

March 8
International Women's Day

March 17
St. Patrick's Day

April 21
Earth Day

Second Sunday in May
Mother's Day

Last Monday before May 25*
Victoria Day

Third Sunday in June
Father's Day

July 1*
Canada Day

First Friday in July
Calgary Stampede

First Monday in August*
Civic Holiday

First Monday in September*
Labor Day

Second Monday in October*
Thanksgiving Day

October 31
Halloween

November 1
All Saints' Day

November 11*
Remembrance Day

December 25*
Christmas Day

December 26*
Boxing Day

Major U.S. Holidays
January 1*

New Year's Day
January 15
Martin Luther King Jr.'s Birthday

Third Monday in January*
Martin Luther King Jr.'s Birthday observed

January 19
Robert E. Lee's Birthday (Southern States)

January 20
Inauguration Day

February 2
Groundhog Day

February 12
Lincoln's Birthday

February 14
Valentine's Day

February 22
Washington's Birthday

APPENDIX B

Third Monday in February*
Washington's Birthday observed

March 17
St. Patrick's Day

March or April
Easter Sunday

April 1
April Fool's Day and Pan American Day

May 1
May Day

Second Sunday in May
Mother's Day

Third Saturday in May
Armed Forces Day

May 30
Memorial Day

Last Monday in May*
Memorial Day observed

June 3
Jefferson Davis' Birthday (Southern States)

June 14
Flag Day

Third Sunday in June
Father's Day

July 4*
Independence Day

First Monday in September*
Labor Day

September 17
Citizenship Day

Fourth Friday in September
Native American Day

October 12
Columbus Day

Second Monday in October*
Columbus Day observed

October 24
United Nations Day

October 31
Halloween

November 11*
Veterans' Day

Fourth Thursday in November*
Thanksgiving Day

December 25*
Christmas Day

*These are the officially designated and observed holidays

Major Foreign Holidays

January

Australia Day on the last Monday

January 1

New Year's Day throughout the Western world and in India, Indonesia, Japan, Korea, the Philippines, Singapore, Taiwan, and Thailand

January 2

Berchtoldstag in Switzerland

January 3

Genshi-Sai (First Beginning), Japan

January 5

Twelfth Night, England

January 6

Epiphany, observed by Catholics throughout Europe and Latin America

January 15

Adult's Day, Japan

January 20

St. Agnes Eve, Great Britain

January-February
Chinese New Year and Vietnamese New Year (Tet)

February
Hamstrom, first Sunday, Switzerland

February 3
Setsubun (Bean-throwing Festival) Japan

February 5
Promulgation of the Constitution Day, Mexico

February 6
New Zealand Day

February 11
National Foundation Day, Japan

February 27
Independence Day, Dominican Republic

March 1
Constitution Day, Panama

March 8
International Women's Day, in U.N., member nations

March 17
St. Patrick's Day, Ireland

March 19
St. Joseph's Day, Colombia, Costa Rica, Italy, Spain

March 21
Benito Juarez's Birthday, Mexico

March 25
Independence Day, Greece
Lady Day (Quarter Day), Great Britain

March 26
Fiesta del Arbol (Arbor Day), Spain

March 29
Youth and Martyrs' Day, Taiwan

March 30
Muslim New Year, Indonesia

APPENDIX B

March-April
Carnival/Lent/Easter: The pre-Lenten celebration of Carnival (Mardi Gras) and the post-Lenten celebration of Easter, Christian countries

April 1
Victory Day, Spain
April Fool's Day, Great Britain

April 5
Arbor Day, Korea

April 6
Van Riebeeck Day, South Africa

April 7
World Health Day, U.N. member nations

April 8
Buddha's Birthday, Korea, Japan
Hana Matsuri (Flower Festival), Japan

April 14
Pan American Day in the Americas

April 19
Declaration of Independence Day, Venezuela

April 22
Queen Isabella Day, Spain

April 23
St. George's Day, England

April 25
Liberation Day, Italy
ANZAC Day, Australia, New Zealand

April 26
Union Day, Tanzania

April 29
Emperor's Day, Japan

April 30
Queen's Birthday, The Netherlands
Walpurgis Night, Germany, Scandinavia

April-May
Independence Day, Israel

May
Constitution Day, first Monday, Japan

May 5
Children's Day, Japan, Korea
Victory of General Zaragosa Day, Mexico
Liberation Day, The Netherlands

May 8
V-E Day, Europe

May 9
Victory over Fascism Day, Commonwealth of Independent States

May 14
Independence Day, Paraguay

May 31
Republic Day, South Africa

June 2
Founding of the Republic Day, Italy

June 5

Constitution Day, Denmark

World Environment Day, U.N. member nations

June 6

Memorial Day, Korea

Flag Day, Sweden

June 8

Muhammad's Birthday, Indonesia

June 10

Portugal Day, Portugal

June 12

Republic Day in the Commonwealth of Independent States

mid-June

Queen's Official Birthday on the second Saturday, Great Britain

June 16

Soweto Day, U.N. member nations

June 20

Flag Day, Argentina

June 29
Feast of Saints Peter and Paul, Chile, Colombia, Costa Rica, Italy, Peru, Spain, Vatican City, Venezuela

July 1
Half-year Holiday, Hong Kong
Bank Holiday, Taiwan

July 5
Independence Day, Venezuela

July 9
Independence Day, Argentina

July 10
Bon (Feast of Fortune), Japan

July 12
Orangemen's Day, Northern Ireland

July 14
Bastille Day, France

mid-July
Feria de San Fermin, second week, Spain

July 17
Constitution Day, Korea

July 18
National Day, Spain

July 20
Independence Day, Colombia

July 21-22
National Holiday, Belgium

July 22
National Liberation Day, Poland

July 24
Simon Bolivar's Birthday, Ecuador, Venezuela

July 25
St. James Day, Spain

July 28-29
Independence Day, Peru

August
Bank Holiday on first Monday, Fiji, Grenada, Guyana, Hong Kong, Ireland, and Malawi

August 1
Lammas Day, England
National Day, Switzerland

August 9
National Day, Singapore

August 10
Independence Day, Ecuador

August 14
Independence Day, Pakistan

August 15
Independence Day, India, Korea,
Assumption Day, Catholic countries

August 16
National Restoration Day, Dominican Republic

August 17
Independence Day, Indonesia

August 31
Independence Day, Trinidad, Tobago

September
Rose of Tralee Festival, Ireland

September 7
Independence Day, Brazil

September 9
Choxo-no-Sekku (Chrysanthemum Day), Japan

September 14
Battle of San Jacinto Day, Nicaragua

mid-September
Sherry Wine Harvest, Spain

September 15
Independence Day, Costa Rica, Guatemala, Nicaragua
Respect for the Aged Day, Japan

September 16
Independence Day, Mexico, Papua New Guinea

September 18-19
Independence Day, Chile

September 28
Confucius' Birthday, Taiwan

Second week of October
Kruger Day, South Africa

October 1
National Day, People's Republic of China
National Holiday, Nigeria

October 2
National Day, People's Republic of China
Mahatma Gandhi's Birthday, India

October 3
National Day, Germany
National Foundation Day, Korea

October 5
Republic Day, Portugal

October 9
Korean Alphabet Day, Korea

October 10
Founding of Republic of China, Taiwan

October 12
Columbus Day, Spain

October 19
Ascension of Muhammad Day, Indonesia

October 20
Revolution Day, Guatemala
Kenyatta Day, Kenya

October 24
United Nations Day, U.N. member nations

October 26
National Holiday, Australia

October 28
Greek National Day, Greece

November 1
All Saints' Day, Catholics in most countries

November 2
All Souls' Day, Ecuador, El Salvador, Luxembourg, Macao, Mexico, San Marino, Uruguay, Vatican City

November 3
Culture Day, Japan

November 4
National Unity Day, Italy

November 5
Guy Fawkes Day, Great Britain

November 11
Armistice Day, Belgium, French Guiana, Tahiti
Veteran's Day, France
Remembrance Day, Bermuda

November 12
Sun Yat-Sen's Birthday, Taiwan

November 15
Proclamation of the Republic Day, Brazil

November 19
National Holiday, Monaco

November 20
Anniversary of the Revolution, Mexico

November 23
Kinro-Kansha-No-Hi (Labor Thanksgiving Day), Japan

November 30
National Heroes' Day, Philippines

December 5
Discovery by Columbus Day, Haiti

December 6
Independence Day, Finland

December 8
Feast of the Immaculate Conception, Catholic countries

December 10
Constitution Day, Thailand
Human Rights Day, U.N. member nations

mid-December
Nine Days of Posada during third week in Mexico

December 25
Christmas Day, Christian countries

December 28
National Day, Nepal

December 31
New Year's Eve throughout the world
Omisoka (Grand Last Day), Japan
Hogmanay Day, Scotland

Appendix C: Websites

Aboriginal Tourism Authority Inc.

http://www.aboriginalnet.com/tourism

Air-Tech

Budget student travel fares offering information on air travel, courier flights, rail travel and car rentals: http://campus.net/trav/airtech/deliver.html

Air Travel/Airlines

Air travel services, airlines, airports, charter services, helicopter tours, air travel http://www.travelmall.com/itm/travel/air/

Alaska Highway News

http://sterlingnews.com/alaska

Alberta Economic Development

http://www.edt.gov.ab.ca/

Alberta Hotel Association

http://www.albertahotels.ab.ca

Alberta Tourism Partnership Corp.

http://www.atp.ab.ca/

Algoma Central Railway Inc.

http://www.mcs.net/~dsdawdy/Canpass/acr/soo_her.html

Assiniboine Park

http://www.mbnet.mb.ca/city/parks/

BC Rail Ltd.

http://www.mcs.net/~dsdawdy/Canpass/ bcr/ bcr.html

B.C. & Yukon Hotels Association

http://www.fleethouse.com/fhcanada/gc-acco.htm

Best Fares

Online magazine with up to the minute budget travel news, special information
for subscribers; http://www.bestfares.com/

Bruce Trail Association

http://www.brucetrail.org/

Budget Travel

Read about this month's travel specials, travelogs, and find agents.
http://www.budgettravel.com/

Calgary Convention & Visitors Bureau

http://www.visitor.calgary.ab.ca/

Canadian Association of Senior Travellers

http://www.seniorsnet.com/cast.htm

Canadian Canoe Association

http://www.openface.ca/paddle/

Canadian Heritage

http://www.pch.gc.ca/

Canadian Heritage-Parks Canada

http://parkscanada.pch.gc.ca

Canadian National Aboriginal Tourism Association

http://www.vli.ca/clients/abc/cnata/cnata3.htm

Canadian Parks & Wilderness Society

http://web.idirect.com/~wildland

Canadian Parks/Recreation Association

http://www.cdnsport.ca/activeliving/cpra.html

Canadian Recreational Canoeing Association

http://www.crca.ca/

Canadian Ski Council

http://www.skican.org

Canadian Tourism Commission

Tourism reference & documentation centre

http://www.info.ic.gc.ca

Canadian Travel Press

http://www.baxter.net

Council Travel

Information about discounted airfares, car rentals, where to stay, Eurailpasses, etc.; http://www.ciee.org/travel/index.htm

Discount Airfares Online

Directory of links to airlines and air travel services offering discount flights. http://www.euro.net/ETN/discount.htm

Discount Tickets Home Page

Links to travel bargains on the web; http://www.etn.nl/dttickets/

Environment Canada

http://www.ec.gc.ca

Eurotrip

Magazine format site with articles on budget travel in Europe

http://www.eurotrip.com/

Fraser Valley Community Information Society

http://mindlink.net/paul_kurucz/vnet.htm

Frugal Travel News

Links to travel resources, tourist offices, transportation and accommodations.

http://www.ftns.com/

Hike Ontario

http://www.freenet.durham.org/hikeon/

Hotelier

http://www.foodservice.ca

International Association for Medical Assistance to Travellers

http://www.sentex.net/~iamat

International Council on Monuments & Sites Canada

http://www.icomos.org/canada

International Special Events Society - Toronto Chapter

http://www.ndgphoenix.com/ises.html

Internet Guide to Hostelling
News and database of hostels worldwide
http://www.hostels.com/

Kootenay Country Tourism Outfitters
http://travel.bc.ca.kootney

Kitchener -Waterloo Oktoberfest
http://www.sentex.net.oktoberfest

London International Airshow
http://www.airshow.org/lias.html

Lonely Planet
A collection of travelogues, travel advisories, and facts about worldwide destinations; http://www.lonelyplanet.com

Manitoba Industry, Trade & Tourism
http://www.gov.mb.ca/manitoba/itt/travel/explore/

Maritime Museum of the Atlantic
www.ednet.ns.ca/educ/museum/mma.html

Ministry of Small Business, Tourism & Culture (British Columbia)
http://www.tbc.gov.bc.ca/homepage.html

Montreal World Film Festival

http://www. ffm-montreal.org/

Nature Canada

http://www.web.apc.org/~cnf

New Brunswick Dept. of Economic Development & Tourism

http://www.gov.nb.ca/edit/index.htm

Newfoundland & Labrador Dept. of Tourism, Culture & Recreation

http://www.gov.nf.ca/tcr/starttcr.htm

Northern Ontario Tourist Outfitters

http://virtualnorth.com/noto/

Nova Scotia Department of Business & Consumer Services

http://www.gov.ns.ca/bacs/

Nunavut Tourism

http://nunanet.com/~nunanet.com

Office des congres et du tourisme due Grand Montreal

http://www.cum.qc.ca/octgm/Welcome.html

Ontario Camping Association

http://www.ontcamp.on.ca

Ontario Federation of Snowmobile Clubs

http://www.transdata.ca/ofsc/index.html

Ontario Ministry of Economic Development, Trade & Tourism

gopher://govonca.gov.on.ca:70/11/medt/english

Ontario Motor Coach Association

http://www.omca.com/

Ontario Out of Doors

http://www.cyberplex.com/fishontario

Ontario Trails Council

http://www.csp.trentu.ca/gomrn/otc.html

Outdoor Recreation Council of B.C.

http://mindlink.net/outrec_council/outrec.htm

Pacific Rim Institute of Tourism

http://www.fleethouse.com/fhcanada/webster/bc/pit-home.htm

Planetarium de Montreal

http://www.planetarium.montreal.qc.ca

Prince Edward Island Depart. of Economic Development & Tourism

http://www.gov.pe.ca/edt/index.html

Quebec North Shore & Labrador Railway Company

http://www.mcs.net/~dsdawdy/Canpass/qnsl/qnsl.html

http://www.cyberplex.com/fishontario

Restaurant & Foodservices Association of British Columbia & The Yukon

http://www.yes.net/RFABCY/

Riding Mountain National Park Visitor Centre

http://parkscanada.pch.gc.ca/parks/manitoba/riding_mountain.htm

.

Saskatchewan Economic Development

http://www.gov.sk.ca/govt/econdev/

The Outpost—Travel Sites

This is the place to check out the Airline schedules, plan a trip via greyhound or, check those train schedules; http://users.deltanet.com/~tdb/travel.htm

Tourism Industry Association of Canada

www.achilles.net/~tiac/homepage.html

Tourism Industry Association of PEI

http://www.gov.pe.ca/conv/tiapei.html

Tourisme Quebec

http://www.gouv.qc.ca/francais/minorg/mto/mto_intro.html

Tourism Victoria/Greater Victoria Visitors & Convention Bureau

http://travel.victoria.bc.ca/

Trail Riders of the Canadian Rockies

http://www.canuck.com/~trcr

Vancouver Coast & Mountains Tourism Region

http://travel.bc.ca

Via Rail Canada Inc.

http://www.mcs.net/~dsdawdy/Campass/via/via.html

Web Guide - Airlines

Directory of airline web pages, online airline reservation services, and sources of discount airfares.http://www.sapphireswan.com/webguide/wg/airlines.htm

Wen-hung Sun's Airlines Page

Travel center, agents, car rental, guides, hotels

http://httpsrv.ocs.drexel.edu/grad/sg95hw7b/airlines.htm

* Note website addresses change often. This list is accurate at date of publication

Important Addresses and Phone Numers

Index

Index

Index